The Anointed

A True Story of Greed, Power and Blind Trust

Dana Gentry

Copyright © 2018

All rights reserved.

Dana Gentry

DEDICATION

To Larry, for giving me the opportunity to produce my greatest accomplishments – our children.

ACKNOWLEDGMENTS

Neither this book nor my career would have been possible if not for a Holy Trinity of journalists – my mentor and longtime boss Bob Stoldal, former Las Vegas Sun managing editor Mike Kelley and the late Ned Day, who once advised a wet-behind-the-ears cub reporter to "follow the money!"

Attorneys Don Campbell, Colby Williams, Maggie McLetchie and the late Mark Hinueber are my heroes. Thank you for your commitment to the First Amendment and the rights of journalists.

Eternal gratitude to the many Aspen Financial investors and other sources who provided information, documents, and inspiration.

To Vicki Quinn, thanks for the tip, Stringer!

To Ashlyn, Beau, Chandler, and Dane—you are my life.

Author's Note

"The best obtainable version of the truth." It's the phrase coined by Carl Bernstein and Bob Woodward to describe the process of reporting one of the biggest stories of the 20th century.

The story contained herein is no Watergate, and I'm certainly no Woodward nor Bernstein.

But like Woodward and Bernstein, I know what it's like to be vilified by the target of an unwelcome investigation.

Bernstein talked at the 2017 White House Correspondents' Dinner about the most infamous attempt in my lifetime to kill the messenger:

"Richard Nixon tried to make the conduct of the press the issue in Watergate instead of the conduct of the president and his men. We tried to avoid the noise and let the reporting speak."

Bernstein's words resonated with me. For almost a decade now, I've tried to let the reporting on Jeff Guinn and Aspen Financial speak for itself while Guinn et al have attempted to divert attention to me.

American politics have undergone cataclysmic change since I began this book. Standard protocols have been eschewed by a president who has proven through word and action to have no use for transparency nor for separating himself from his family's business interests.

The public has a right to know about the finances of the people who aspire to the highest offices in the land. Donald Trump isn't the first elected official to attempt to hide his interests. In a clumsy, ham-handed fashion, he may be more transparent than others. Trump even

The Anointed Son

wondered aloud on the campaign trail whether a family-administered trust could, indeed, be considered "blind."

Conflicts of interest in politics are nothing new, though the current president's entanglements rival any we've witnessed in modern America.

Those we know of will be thoroughly digested and regurgitated by the national media. But it's the conflicts of which we are unaware that pose the greatest threat to our democracy, that threaten the fleeting yet essential hope that our vote means something—that our elected leaders will be who they hold themselves out to be.

As a longtime journalist, I've developed a healthy cynicism and a chronic disdain for politicians. But former Nevada Governor Kenny Guinn appeared to me and others to be one of the good guys.

Unlike many governors, Guinn earned the respect of lawmakers and citizens from both sides of the aisle, often infuriating his own Republican colleagues with his common sense, bipartisan approach to solving the state's problems.

In 2003, when Governor Guinn sought to increase taxes, the right wing of his own party in the Legislature revolted. Rather than kowtow, Guinn defended his position, fighting all the way to the State Supreme Court. That was the kind of leader Nevadans had in Kenny Guinn.

Thanks to Guinn's primary legacy, the Guinn Millennium Scholarship, thousands of Nevada students, including my own children, have had the financial burden of higher education lessened by $10,000.

Respected educator, businessman and governor. That is the how Guinn is remembered.

Even today, eight years after his wife, Dema, found her husband dead on the ground, the apparent victim of a fall from their roof, Guinn remains one of the most respected public officials in the state. A public policy think tank bears his name.

Kenny Guinn was one of the good guys. That's what I thought. As it turns out, he was simply more elegant at concealment than the oafish Donald Trump.

The revelations in these pages about not only Jeff Guinn, but his father, the governor, will not win me any popularity contests, and are likely to initiate another effort to destroy my credibility. As you'll read, I was accused in legal documents back in 2009 by Jeff Guinn and his hired guns of being a reporter for sale—of accepting money, gifts, and favors in exchange for producing stories on Jeff Guinn and Aspen Financial.

The truth is I did not then, nor have I ever, accepted anything in exchange for doing stories. Jeff Guinn's efforts to subpoena information from me went all the way to the Nevada Supreme Court.

In 2015, I briefly did freelance investigative work for attorney Dennis Prince. I am disclosing this information in the hopes that readers will take in the sworn testimony and public records on which this book is largely based, and decide for themselves whether my brief employment compromises the credibility of the information.

Like Woodward and Bernstein, I hope to avoid the noise and let the reporting speak.

PREFACE

My former colleague Jon Ralston wrote a book almost twenty years ago in which he detailed the rise of a first-time candidate guided by the state's most formidable political forces to Nevada's most powerful position: governor.

The candidate—a handsome, affable man's man named Kenny Guinn, worked his way from the Clark County School District to the board rooms of some of the state's largest corporations. With the help of the casino industry, political consultant Sig Rogich (who gave up his own gubernatorial aspirations to play kingmaker), and public relations executive Pete Ernaut (who would eventually become Guinn's Chief of Staff), Guinn trounced his opposition and won two terms.

Governor Kenny Guinn, a political neophyte, found himself at the helm of the fastest growing state in the nation, overseeing the biggest growth spurt in Nevada history—a time when tourism flourished, real estate values ballooned by double digits, and consumption at all levels became more conspicuous almost by the minute.

The median price of a home in Las Vegas sailed to new heights during Guinn's term, from about $140,000 when he took office in 1999 to $315,000 at its peak in June of 2006, Guinn's final year as governor.[1]

I'm no economist, but even a casual observer like me could see the writing on the wall. With incomes growing annually at maybe two to three percent and home prices skyrocketing by fifty percent, something had to give. Nevada was ripe for a long fall when the bubble inevitably burst, ultimately pierced by the collapse of the mortgage-

---

[1] Standard & Poor's/Case-Shiller Home Price Indices

backed securities market.

The residential market was not alone during the boom.

Applied Analysis, a Las Vegas business consultant, reports the price of off-Strip raw land peaked in 2007 at $939,357 an acre, up dramatically from pre-bubble values that fetched less than $40,000 an acre in undeveloped areas of the valley.[2]

Within a few years, prices soared, thanks in part to brokerages such as Jeff Guinn's Aspen Financial. Owned by the governor's son, Aspen was willing to finance sums well above appraised value to valley homebuilders (and pocket the lucrative origination fees).

Many of those builders designated Jeff Guinn's other company, Aspen Mortgage, as their preferred lender, and sent prospective buyers Guinn's way.

In 2005, developer and Aspen borrower John Ritter's Focus Property Group paid an unheard of $300,000 an acre for 1,700 acres in the northwest Las Vegas valley.

Then, as quickly as the bubble inflated, it burst.

Deafening silence replaced the raucous bidding that had become common at federal land auctions.

Properties throughout the Las Vegas valley rode the wave of artificially inflated values, only to plunge deeply underwater.

Homes that just months earlier reaped multiple sale offers above asking price now sat on the market for months. "For Sale" signs that lined residential streets were quickly replaced with "Foreclosure" signs.

Borrowers with adjustable rate mortgages, who relied on lender promises of refinances, walked away or waited it out until the banks eventually caught up.

---

[2] Las Vegas Review-Journal March 7, 2010 *Recession Leaves Raw Land in Dust*

The Anointed Son

Eviction services replaced real estate as the growth industry.

Today, a decade later, Southern Nevada's real estate recovery has lagged behind the rest of the nation. But it's catching up.

Looking back, you'd think a guy like Kenny Guinn, a walking calculator and banking icon, would have seen the fall coming. Maybe he did. Maybe he sensed the bubble inflating dangerously beyond its means.

Maybe he imagined the precipice, the avalanche of homes about to tumble into the abyss, the years buried under water, and the lives ruined by all that greed.

Maybe in his mind's eye, Nevada's governor anticipated the neighborhoods in collapse.

Maybe Kenny Guinn knew that audits would soon reveal the state's mortgage division was woefully inadequate, "regulating" what was about to become Ground Zero in a national lending crisis that precipitated the Great Recession.[3]

Maybe he feared the bust would expose a variety of Ponzi-like schemes flourishing in Nevada.

Perhaps Kenny Guinn recognized that his own son's empire, in which the governor had millions of dollars invested via a "blind trust," was cutting corners and at risk of exposure if subjected to greater scrutiny and stricter regulation.

Aspen Financial Services stood on a foundation of trust deed-backed loans secured by "appraised-as-if-completed" properties, propped up by equity-eroding terms that earned Jeff Guinn a seemingly never-ending stream of lending fees. The hard money lender estimates brokering $300 to $400 million in loans a year from 2000 to 2006, while his father governed the state, with some years as high as $400 to $440

---

[3] *Nevada Appeal*, Dec. 2008 *Audit sharply criticizes Mortgage Lending Division*

million.[4]

But they weren't always new loans. Jeff Guinn was engaged in serial refinancing of the same properties, churning deal after deal, creating one loan to make payments on another, and attaching ever-inflating appraisals.

Jeff Guinn, with the help of Governor Guinn's substantial and undisclosed investment in an industry regulated by the state, was feeding an insatiable beast. It was a cycle of greed that would eventually be laid bare by the crash.

Whatever he knew about the impending crisis or the unsustainable increase in both residential and commercial real estate prices, Kenny Guinn—the respected numbers man—did nothing to head off the wave of defaults about to engulf his state and catapult Nevada to the top of the foreclosure heap.

In 2008, with the Silver State already leading the nation in foreclosures for eighteen months, Guinn's successor, Jim Gibbons, a man Guinn held in low regard, held a pow-wow with the state's biggest banks and mortgage lenders.[5]

By then, the damage was done. Home values had plunged by as much as fifty percent from their 2006 peak. Commercial property was about to follow suit.

Governor Guinn's son, who boasted to the media before the recession of never having filed a foreclosure, was about to suffer a reversal of fortune, taking down hundreds of investors in his wake, among them his parents—the Governor and First Lady.

Jeff Guinn was about to become not only the defendant in a spate of

---

[4] Jeff Guinn Deposition #1 p. 135
[5] Officials to Talk Foreclosures, LVRJ, November 22, 2008

The Anointed Son

civil lawsuits, but also the target of a federal criminal probe.

This is the story of Jeff Guinn's ambition and the lengths he went to achieve it, how his father gamed the trust vested in the governor by the people of Nevada, and how the two compromised the Guinn name in pursuit of a buck.

It's a story of drugs, money, corruption, and family dysfunction.

My former colleague, Jon Ralston, titled his book about Kenny Guinn *The Anointed One*.

This is the rest of the story. *The Anointed Son*.

I always told Ralston there will be one big difference between our books. Mine will sell.

1: THE BUSINESS MODEL

Attorney Dennis Prince: Is it your opinion, based upon everything that you reviewed, that there was a scheme to defraud by Jeff Guinn and Aspen...?

Aspen Investor Charles Thompson: The simple answer to that is yes. But like most criminals, I think they thought they would never get caught.

October 4, 2010

Charles Thompson Deposition

Ruthe v. Aspen P 49

By the late '90s, the Mob had been excised from the Las Vegas Strip. The Skim, which funneled millions of dollars during a span of decades to half a dozen or so Mafia families, was but a memory, perhaps best preserved for the masses in Martin Scorsese's mob saga, *Casino*.

But a new type of Syndicate was taking hold. While mobsters siphoned coin voluntarily forsaken by casino patrons, this shyster targeted unwitting victims, hoodwinked by the promise of safe, secure investments.

The hard money lender was the darling of developers out to make a quick buck during Southern Nevada's real estate boom. The Savings and Loan crisis, in which financiers such as Charles Keating purchased banks, used them as piggy banks, and made bad loans to borrowers with no skin in the game, prompted a flood of regulation that made borrowing from those institutions much more onerous. But hard money was easy to find—more expensive than a bank, but quicker and requiring less documentation.

Hard money loans provided investors, who pooled their money to finance multi-million dollar projects, with double-digit returns and the security of real estate as collateral. The investor-backed loans gave borrowers with no equity a route to financing. And they proved a boon for the middleman—the broker—who got paid to underwrite the deals and pair the investors with the borrowers.

Aspen Financial opened in 1995, granting short-term loans—generally one year or eighteen months—to some of Southern Nevada's biggest developers. Loan summaries presented to potential investors noted six-month extensions were available "as long as there has been no deterioration of the borrower's financial condition and all payments have been made as agreed."[6]

That caveat, it would occur to me, was a canard, since the borrower's interest payments—in almost all cases—were wrapped into the loan and impounded at closing. In other words, the payment history was carved in stone from the close of escrow. With the payments guaranteed, the borrower's credit and financial standing were irrelevant. Despite this, Aspen's loan officers would tout borrowers with good credit and payment histories when pitching investments.

Jim Zeller, an Aspen investor and escrow and title professional with forty years of experience, admitted in a deposition in one of the many lawsuits that would eventually be filed against Jeff Guinn's company that he never realized he and other investors were making the payments for the borrowers.

Attorney Dennis Prince: For example, when she (Aspen's loan officer) would contact you after a loan matured, did she comment typically on the borrower in the prospective transaction, that they always made their payments, we've had long history with Aspen, that type of thing?
Zeller: Yes. That's true.
Q: Would she typically vouch for them being a good borrower, for lack of a better term?
A: I remember her saying they've always made their payments.

---

[6]Aspen Financial Loan Summary

Q: Retrospectively...
A: Retrospectively, they made it out of my money.[7]

Jeff Guinn, under questioning from plaintiffs' attorney Dennis Prince, in one of the many lawsuits that would besiege Aspen Financial, testified in deposition that the loans he brokered had the payments built into it.

Attorney Dennis Prince: What steps would you take to inform investors about interest reserve?

Jeff Guinn: If it was in the loan brief, Dennis, and they wanted to ask a question, they could ask a question, what is interest reserve.[8]

It was a good deal for borrowers, who could buy or develop property using OPM—Other People's Money. With the payments rolled into the loan, the risk of default was nil. Sure, the need for serial refinancing to sometimes generate future interest reserves tended to erode equity, but in a booming market with skyrocketing values, it was a risk neither borrowers or lenders considered. Not all understood that Jeff Guinn's fees eroded the lenders' equity with every refinance.

It was a great deal for Aspen. Jeff Guinn got his origination fees, two percent for First Deeds of Trust, and three to three-and-a-half percent for Second Priority Deeds, not to mention servicing fees (usually three-eighths of a percent of the loan, according to Aspen VP Elaine Elliot's sworn testimony).

An expert witness hired by two of Aspen's biggest investors, Donna and Chuck Ruthe, would later find that on the roughly two dozen loans at issue in the Ruthe litigation alone, Aspen's estimated fees totaled more than $14 million dollars.[9]

Aspen also pocketed loan extension fees, even though the broker's

---

[7] Jim Zeller deposition, Ruthe v. Guinn, December 14, 2010 Page 30
[8] Jeff Guinn Deposition #1 p. 147
[9] Bruce Coin expert report Ruthe v. Guinn

loan agreement clearly states those fees were to be paid to the lender/investors.[10]

The Aspen Business Model was not such a great deal for investors, many of whom admit now that they were lulled into a false sense of security by the Guinn name or their personal relationships with Kenny and Dema, not to mention the portrait of the governor hanging in Aspen's office.

In 2008, Aspen investor Donna Ruthe, who along with her husband Chuck would later sue Aspen and Jeff Guinn, testified in another lawsuit that Jeff Guinn told her he intentionally engaged in prominent name-dropping, including that of Ruthe's husband, when pitching loans to potential investors.

A: That was actually Jeff Guinn said that directly to me, that, you know -- there were certain people... He would say, "Well, Chuck is in the deal." He said, "I love having Chuck in a deal" because — -- he said, "I just saw him. Chuck Ruthe is in this deal." So I know that directly from a comment said from Mr. Guinn.

Q: I guess, did Mr. Guinn believe that if Chuck Ruthe was in a deal, that it added credibility to the transaction or to whatever he was trying to do at that time?

Guinn Attorney BRUCE WILLOUGHBY: I'm going to object as speculation. Vague and ambiguous.

Q: (BY MR. PRINCE) Based upon your observation, is that your belief?

A: Based upon my observation, I would say yes. But Mr. Guinn would talk further about it with me, saying he — -- it was good having Chuck's name in the deal.

---

[10] Aspen Loan Agreement Section 7.18.(b) On or before the original maturity date, Borrower shall pay Lender an extension fee in immediately available funds in the amount of one-half of one percent...

Q: Why?

A: He said he also used Kenny Guinn. He would say his dad is in the deal.[11]

With Las Vegas investors still reeling from the mid-'90s collapse of a high-profile hard money brokerage, Jeff Guinn and Aspen employees turned name-dropping into a brilliant marketing strategy, according to the testimony of investors.

MaryAnn Arminio says her husband was investing with Del Mar Mortgage, a company owned by broker Mike Shustek, when his investment counselor Jennifer Schai left to work for Aspen.

Arminio testified in the Ruthes' suit against Guinn that it was the governor's connection to the company that attracted her to Aspen.

Attorney Dennis Prince: Did Jennifer tell you who she was going to work for? Other than it was Aspen, did she tell you it was Jeff Guinn?

MaryAnn Arminio: Yes, exactly. She said that the company that she was moving to, it was involved with Kenny Guinn, which is the governor of Nevada. So it's very reputable.

Q: Did you place trust and confidence in Jennifer's statements that this is, the governor's son owns Aspen, so therefore they're going to operate appropriately and professionally and with integrity?

A: That's what gave us the most confidence of moving over to Aspen.[12]

Jim Zeller says he and his wife invested with Aspen after his wife lost money with another hard money lender. Zeller testified under oath that he got a sense of security and a level of comfort in knowing Jeff Guinn and family were investing in the loans.

---

[11] Donna Ruthe deposition, Ruthe v. Guinn, January 11, 2008 P. 42
[12] Mary Ann Arminio deposition, Ruthe v. Guinn, August 16, 2012 p. 11

"Well, I considered that a positive. ...he's controlling the show. And if he's putting his money in it, it should be a good deal."[13]

Donna Ruthe, a real estate broker, testified in a 2013 deposition that she had no experience investing in trust deeds prior to a pitch then-governor Kenny Guinn made to Ruthe and her husband, Chuck, shortly after Guinn took office.

Ruthe says the governor, who wanted to thank the couple for their help during the election, arranged a lunch in 1999 at Rosemary's, a popular Las Vegas eatery.

Donna Ruthe: ... former Governor Kenny Guinn suggested investing in his son's company and make sure we went on loans that he was on and all the borrowers were strong and Jeff made sure they were good borrowers, I had a real clear head to write that check because I trusted Kenny Guinn and I trusted his son because it was his son. And that's my experience.

I can tell you that he talked about the borrowers, how strong they were, the comfort, the money he had in there, his son's company, he was overseeing it, and they were top borrowers here in town, and, of course, it's going to be trust deeds on the property. ... But he was just discussing–they were talking about land prices, and Chuck retiring because Chuck had just retired from Boyd a few years earlier. And just that Chuck should think about getting rid of all the pressure of all the land and everything and put the money where he could put it with his son and they'd be overseeing it.
... And Kenny said that he was putting a lot of money he was making and had in there, and it was great getting a check every month than sweating it out waiting for something else.[14]

Donna Ruthe testified in 2013 about another conversation with Governor Guinn in 2005, in the parking lot of Aspen's West Sahara

---

[13] Jim Zeller deposition, Ruthe v. Guinn, December 14, 2010 p. 24

[14] *Donna Ruthe 2013 deposition p. 190*

office building in Las Vegas.

A: ... And his security guy was outside. And we stopped and we talked and just started talking about the loans... He specifically said – he said, how are you doing. I said, we're doing good. The checks always came on time. And he said, well, you don't have to worry. Then he repeated that. He said, I'm always here. You could always call me. I kind of oversee what's going on. Not to worry. And he goes, you know, I'm here all the time. He said, I have my office. When I retire, I'll be in there full time.[15]

"Kenny was there, bigger than life, when I went to Aspen. It was always Kenny, not Jeff. Finally, I thought, an honest hard money lender," investor Vickie Valdov told me during a 2015 interview. "Kenny and Dema were on all the loans. Who thought anything could go wrong investing with the governor?"

Sharing an investment with the Guinns provided a great sense of security to other lenders. But what most didn't know, from Aspen's inception Kenny and Dema Guinn's money rarely remained invested for the duration of a loan. Jeff Guinn often used his parents' money like a line of credit, filling the gap to close another loan and generate another origination fee for Aspen. Sometimes within a matter of hours, days or weeks of buying an interest in a loan, Aspen would sell Kenny and Dema's shares to the next investor.

Wash. Rinse. Repeat.

Charles Thompson was a former Clark County Assistant District Attorney. In his private practice Thompson represented Lawyer's Title, sometimes suing hard money lenders. To say Thompson knew his way around an escrow and title file is an understatement. Thompson began investing with Aspen Financial in 1998.

In 2010 Thompson was deposed in a lawsuit filed against Jeff Guinn by

---

[15] Donna Ruthe 2013 deposition, p. 199

the Ruthes. Thompson testified at the time that all fourteen of his Aspen investor-backed loans were non-performing. The monthly interest payments that previously arrived like clockwork had ceased.

One of the Ruthes' attorneys, Joel Hansen, asked Thompson about his decision to close his private practice.

Q: Did you feel at that point in 2005 with your investments through Aspen that you were financially comfortable such that you could retire?

A Yeah.

Q Did that factor into your decision-making when you left the practice of law, these investments you had through Aspen totaling in excess of a million dollars were fully performing?

A Yes.

Q Was that an important factor in your decision-making when you stopped practicing?

A Well, yes. If I would have known what was going to happen, I would have done it differently.[16]

How did someone with Thompson's background willingly turn over much of his life savings to Aspen? It's a question Thompson says plagued him.

A: See, I've been bothered by how did myself and these people and so many others get sucked into what we got sucked into. Because we're supposed to be smarter than this. So I've spent a lot of time figuring out how it happened. Because what I'm going to tell you, what I've said to you is how I got into it. I walked right into it. But there was created, in the beginning and throughout this, an attitude of feeling, an environment, almost like an anesthetic in which you could trust the Guinns. And I sat back and analyzed that and diagnosed it, how and

---

[16] Charles Thompson Deposition p. 10

why. Because there's so many reasons that I can sit here today and tell you that had I known, I would have bailed out immediately. And why didn't I know with my experience? Why didn't these two people know? I've talked to many other people. I thought -

MR. HANSEN: For the record, you mean Donna and Chuck when you say "these people"?

THE WITNESS: I'm talking about Donna and Chuck, who also had experience. Kenny Gragson, who was in real estate, businessman. I've talked to lots of people. And none of us were aware. So how did it happen? I say none of us. There was probably two, three, less than five percent had a knowledge or belief about some things.

So I just tried to analyze it. And your questions point out something to me. And that is that this environment of trust that was in fact imposed upon us had certain elements to it. And it was very clever, by retrospect, it was very clever, it was very organized. It was master manipulation. And it was done in an attempt to leave no doubt in our mind as to trust. And that was, "Before I got off the phone, I was reminded that the owner of the company was the state of Nevada's governor's son." And that was instrumental in them making the decision.

Q So you're saying someone from Aspen would tell these investors that Jeff Guinn was the governor's son?

A Yes.

Q And that you believe that was all in an attempt to create an environment.

A It was part of it. It was part of it.

Q Okay.

A That you had this feeling of security and trust. But there are other parts of it that were put together and that I consider significant. And

The Anointed Son

that is that secondly, Kenny Guinn's presence involving Aspen existed. What I mean is ultimately, he had an office there. That Jeff bragged about it. ...[17]

...in addition to that, you had something else happening during this time. And that is when we received, ultimately and inevitably, our gold and green booklets, the so-called opening and closing packages, those were received, in my memory, always after the loan closed.

When we received those, one of the things some of us used to do was turn to Exhibit As, to see who else had invested. And there you would find, generally on the first couple pages you would find something involving the Guinn family. Jeff, Kenny, and/or Aspen employees, and Aspen were investors.

So you take that and you add it to the fact that Kenny was -- and Kenny had developed at that time a reputation. And some good things can be said about his reputation and his abilities. Kenny Guinn was a charismatic man. He was a very smart man. He was gregarious. He was smooth. And handled himself well. And with that came this reputation...[18]

Hard money was a risky industry fraught with high-profile failures. Thompson, Valdov, Zeller, the Ruthes and others knew the risks, but they reassured themselves, if the governor is on board, it must be safe.

With double-digit interest payments arriving like clockwork each month and the economy booming, many investors gave little thought to the cash they invested with Jeff Guinn, whom they paid and trusted to look out for their interests.

Were they too trusting? Who wouldn't be? The governor's son boasted to a newspaper reporter of not even a single foreclosure, but left out the fact that the payments were rolled into the loans and impounded

---

[17] Thompson p. 30 - 33

[18] Thompson p. 33

at the close of escrow.

Default was nearly impossible—as long as the stream of new money to fund another loan and the next round of payments never ran dry.

David Moody is a bank executive who briefly worked at Aspen in the mid-2000s. His 2010 deposition in a lawsuit against Guinn illustrates the schizophrenia that gripped not only Aspen, but much of the lending community at the time.

Attorney Dennis Prince: Mr. Moody, isn't it true one of the reasons when you're making loans you're looking at the quality of the borrower, the type of collateral, you're always looking at the worst-case scenario? That's the point of it; correct?
David Moody: Correct. ....
Q: Did you ever become concerned that—with Aspen's business model, that if there's any downturn in the economy, that it would cause a failure of Aspen?
A: No.
Q: You never felt that way?
A: No
Q: Did you ever feel that it's the investors who at the end are the ones left holding the bag? If there's any turn down in the economy or if you can't get new money to refinance one of existing—
A: No. Because the economy was so strong, we didn't think about that.[19]

---

[19] David Moody deposition, 2010, Ruthe v. Guinn. p. 78

2: SELF-MADE MAN

"Tell the love story Kenny had with the state," Dema Guinn said between tears and sobs.

*"He cared so much about the people of Nevada; he cared about the people who couldn't make their house payments, people who couldn't put food on the table, seniors, children. Every morning and night he worried about the state." -*Dema Guinn to Las Vegas Review-Journal columnist Jane Ann Morrison in 2010

Kenny Guinn was a child of The Dust Bowl, his family uprooted from its native Arkansas by the violent wind storms that defined a decade and sent the dispossessed packing by the hundreds of thousands.

Guinn's mother, Vergie, had a third-grade education. His illiterate father crammed his wife and children in the family car and escaped Arkansas for California during the depression. A biography written by the Associated Press's Brendan Riley in 1999 recounts Guinn's early experiences living in poverty, being bullied by other children, and his early success as an athlete.

He recalls living with his parents, older brother and two younger sisters in a poor area near Exeter, Calif., and facing prejudice toward "Okies" and "Arkies." But he also remembers wanting to move up and out, and the way that people in Exeter helped him do that.

Help came in many forms, including a job pumping gas and another family's home in Exeter where he stayed during the school year while his parents picked fruit elsewhere.

"I knew full well I wanted to do something besides what my family had been doing all those years," he says.

"Once I got into athletics, I became very competitive in school and things in general in my life," he says. "And I felt I could do whatever it *was that I took off to do."*[20]

And he did—amassing more than $5 million in personal wealth, according to that 1999 biography.

Kenny Guinn told a journalist he enjoyed reading biographies of successful people to learn how captains of industry came by their gains. In 1998, Guinn put his own success story into play.

Here's how political reporter Jon Ralston captured the moment in his book.

Guinn was the epitome of the Nevada establishment. Not only was he a regular honoree as man of the year for some civic group, but he was a board member of Boyd Gaming and Del Webb, representing the most powerful (gaming) and second most powerful (development) industries in the state.

He had spent three and a half decades in Las Vegas preparing for this moment -- serving Republican and Democratic governors as chairman of blue-ribbon panels, appearing on television as the helmsman of various bond campaigns for more schools and policemen, and achieving financial security after stints as chairman of a utility, Southwest Gas, and a bank, Nevada Savings. He had cultivated an amiable and dedicated persona, one that seemed to reflect the motto of the bank he once served -- Big, Safe, and Friendly.

—The Anointed One, Jon Ralston

"Big, Safe, and Friendly." It was an image Guinn and his son Jeff would bank on to lure investors to lend via Aspen Financial.

---

[20] Biography of Kenny Guinn, Brendan Riley, Associated Press, January 1999

3: IN KENNY WE TRUST

"I believe that his reputation for honor and integrity was a myth. That's as I sit here today. At that time, I didn't believe that. ...As I sit here today, I believe his reputation was a myth. But there was more than that. At that time, it was strong. It was built around Kenny Guinn. It was sold around Kenny Guinn." –Aspen Investor/Lender Charles Thompson, Deposition October 4, 2010 p. 34

Financial disclosure laws exist to make the public aware of potential conflicts of interest that could be perceived to compromise the integrity of elected officials. The conflict doesn't have to be real. Even the perception of a conflict is to be avoided.

Nevada's financial disclosure form, completed by candidates and incumbents alike, requires disclosure of all income, business interests, and real estate in Nevada or adjacent states in which a candidate or official holds an ownership or beneficial interest.[21]

Kenny Guinn was already a seasoned investor in mortgage-backed trust deeds when his son Jeff opened Aspen Financial Services, a mortgage brokerage, in 1995. By the time Kenny Guinn ran for governor in 1998, public records reveal the elder Guinn and his wife, Dema, had invested in dozens of loans brokered by their son's company.[22]

Candidate Guinn's initial financial disclosure form, filed June 2, 1998,

---

[21] NRS 281.571
[22] Clark County Public Records

listed Aspen Financial and Developers of Nevada, a company owned by former City of Las Vegas Manager Russell Dorn and developer Roland Sturm, as sources of income.

Candidate Guinn's disclosure made no mention of his beneficial interest in the seventeen trust deed loans he funded during the reporting period—twelve of them to borrowers who also happened to be contributors to his first campaign.

Public records reveal that in the eight years Guinn was in office, the First Couple funded a cumulative face amount of $36 million in more than 300 loans brokered by their son, Jeff.

I would come to learn there was more than a casual intersection of Aspen borrowers and Guinn campaign contributors.

The loans Kenny Guinn funded through his son's company posed a quandary for the new governor.

Disclosing them, some of which he held for only hours or days, would not only be a logistical nightmare to report, but would surely draw scrutiny from at least the media, if not mortgage regulators and ethics buffs.

To liquidate his investments with Aspen Financial and place the funds in traditional holdings would prove costly, not only to Kenny Guinn, who was inclined to augment his modest government salary with the double-digit returns trust deed investments offered, but also for his son, Jeff, who used his parents' millions as a piggy bank to fund larger loans and earn increasingly lucrative origination fees for his company.

Governor Guinn's answer to the disclosure dilemma: The Guinn Irrevocable Asset Management Trust, formed on March 30, 1999 *"for the purpose of managing assets and making investments without disclosure to the Grantors of the nature of the investments made so as to avoid the appearance of a conflict of interest by Kenny Guinn in executing the Office of Governor of the State of Nevada."*

Kenny Guinn first disclosed the existence of the blind trust the same day it was formed—March 30, 1999—the day the new governor signed and filed his second financial disclosure form.

What the governor failed to disclose was that the co-trustees of the "blind trust" would be his sons, Jeff and Steve.

Because Nevada, unlike many other states, has no laws prohibiting relatives from administering blind trusts of public officials, Jeff Guinn was able to put his parents' money to work for his state-regulated company.

It was a win-win for the Guinns and their son, the hard money broker.

The First Couple's investments proved invaluable to Aspen Financial.[23] The sight of the Guinn Irrevocable Asset Management Trust on the list of co-investors, which was provided to beneficiaries of a loan upon close of escrow, gave Kenny Guinn's fellow Aspen investors a keen sense of security.

In a state bereft of laws governing blind trusts, and with his investments shielded, the likable and seemingly trustworthy Kenny Guinn was able to conceal his assets, loan money to campaign contributors via his son's brokerage, and significantly augment his income while being a public servant, all without scrutiny.

But everything I knew indicated Kenny Guinn regularly discussed Aspen's loans with other investors.

So how blind was Kenny's trust?

With the exception of his initial financial disclosure, filed June 2, 1998, Guinn's filings make no mention of his assorted business relationship with Aspen Financial.

While governor, Kenny Guinn appears to have personally guaranteed a $4.7 million loan from Community Bank of Nevada. The proceeds were

---

[23] Clark County Public Records

used for Aspen Financial's office building on West Sahara in Las Vegas.[24]

Guinn failed to note the indebtedness and his interest in the real estate on his 2005, 2006, and 2007 financial disclosures filed with the Secretary of State.

According to federal court records, Kenny Guinn was a principal of Coronado Aspen II, LLC, the entity that received $210,000 a year in rent paid by Aspen Financial. The lease agreement would become public record, filed in federal court documents.

The governor was not only a multimillion-dollar investor in his son's company, he was also secretly its landlord.

With an office at Aspen Financial, an interest in the company (both as its landlord and guarantor of the loan secured by its office building), and his sons as co-trustees, I wondered whether Governor Guinn was even slightly myopic, let alone truly "blind" to his investments.

The truth would become crystal clear: the Guinn Irrevocable Asset Management Trust—the governor's blind trust—left Nevadans, not the governor, in the dark.

---

[24] Guinn v. Community Bank, April 9, 2009, p. 16

4: FAST FRIENDS

I met Jeff and Monica Guinn through my friend since high school, Vicki Quinn. Vicki is married to a contractor named Steve Quinn. He's a New Yorker who came to Las Vegas in the late 1970s to find fortune. He found Vicki Steward in a bar one night and took her home, and she never left.

The Quinns have a history of becoming fast friends with other couples and striking up deep friendships that quickly fizzle. I was not at all surprised when Vicki and her husband forged a rapid bond with Monica Guinn and her husband, Jeff. And I was equally nonplussed when the friendship ended. But this time, the fizzle provided fodder for what would become one of the biggest stories of my career. I'd be followed, surveilled, and hauled before the Nevada Supreme Court.

Monica Guinn and Vicki Quinn have similar last names. That's where the likeness ends. The two are as different as could be.

Vicki is short, struggles with her weight, and talks like a truck driver. She's always the life of the party, even more so before she got sober. Monica is a tall, soft-spoken blonde. Indeed, she is so soft-spoken, I often struggled to hear her almost-whispered words.

The two met at Our Lady of Las Vegas, where their children attended parochial school. Monica soon joined Vicki in a prayer group arranged by our mutual friend, Delise Fertitta Sartini, the daughter of local casino pioneer Frank Fertitta.

Jeff Guinn embraced the Quinns as though they were family. He enlisted Vicki Quinn as a confidante and hired her husband's contracting services for his building projects.

The two couples dined with Governor Guinn and the First Lady, and the Guinns lavished gifts on the Quinns and their children, including season tickets to UNLV Runnin' Rebel basketball games for the Quinns' wheelchair-bound son, Stephen.

The Quinns loved socializing with the First Family of Nevada. They took trips, flew in the Guinn plane to campaign events with the governor, who was seeking a second term, and attended exclusive events.

Above all, for years, they kept the Guinn family secrets.

5: THE PILL PROBLEM

Steve Quinn testified in a 2013 deposition that he first met Jeff Guinn at a UNLV football game in 2000.

Q: And how did you meet?
A: He was introduced to me. As he shook my hand, he had two Lortabs in it and handed me two Lortabs. ...
Q: And what did you do with those Lortabs?
A: I probably ate one of them. I don't know what I did with the other... [25]

...

Q: You said you were aware that there have been some allegations made about Mr. Guinn's narcotic drug use. Are you aware of the details of those allegations or just the fact that he was using them?
A: I'm fairly aware. I wound up checking him into a rehab hospital. ... I received a phone call from my wife who was over at the Guinn residence with Mrs. Guinn and with Dr. Green, and I received a phone call to come on over to help because things were not going too well.
Q: What do you mean "Things were not going too well?"
A: Whether or not Jeff was suicidal or whether or not -- they needed help. [26] *...*
Q: Why did you decide to help?
A: He was a friend
Q: Was your wife involved with that as well?
A: She was there, yes... She was in holding his head on her chest, stroking his hair, telling him that everything would be fine.
Q: Were you using narcotics at that point in time.

---

[25] Stephen Quinn deposition 2/27/13 p. 17 - 18
[26] Quinn p. 20

A: No

Q: Do you know how Mr. Guinn had obtained these narcotics that you are referring to?

A: No I don't.

Q: You never supplied him any?

A: No.

Q: Did there come a point in time where your relationship with Mr. and Mrs. Guinn went downhill?

A: Yes

Q: Was it shortly after that?

A: Yes.

Q: What happened?

A: It just-- Jeff started making some claims to the Contractor Board about me, and it just disintegrated from that point.[27]

That was an understatement. Quinn would be sued, his home and business surveilled, and his family followed -- all at the direction of the governor's son.

---

[27] Quinn p. 27-28

6: THE INVESTORS

Although I never invested a penny with Jeff Guinn's Aspen Financial, my research would reveal a long list of investors I've known for years.

Aspen's investors ranged from the very wealthy to retirees or others on fixed incomes hoping to eke a little more interest from their savings than they could earn from a bank.

Las Vegas, despite its growth, remains a small town.

In 2015, I had lunch with Gabrielle Barel, a childhood friend I hadn't seen in years. I mentioned I was writing a book about a hard money lender. Did she know what that was, I inquired?

"Aspen?" she asked. I nodded, surprised she had heard of it.

"I lost money with Aspen," she said. "My dad did, too."

Gabrielle's dad, Marcel Barel, was the ski instructor at Lee Canyon, the only snow skiing facility in Southern Nevada for decades. If you grew up in Las Vegas and took ski lessons, it was probably at Marcel's Ski Skool. For the half-century I've known him, Gabby's father has lived a frugal existence in a mountain cabin without electricity. I believe he has recently embraced such amenities.

Gabby didn't know what loans she and her dad were on, just that the economy tanked and they lost their money.

Gabby was probably among the majority of Aspen investors who never understood how they lost their money, just that it was gone. After all, the economy fell apart. Investments have risks, you know.

Gidget Grittini became a single parent of two boys when her husband passed away. Grittini invested her husband's life insurance proceeds with Aspen Financial. When the loans in which she invested went bad and Aspen Financial failed to foreclose, Grittini's sons were forced to drop out of college.

Even after almost a decade of investigating Aspen Financial, hearing countless stories of people who lost their life savings, the thought of Marcel and Gabby losing their money and of Grittini's boys being forced to abandon their educations makes the losses endured by them and thousands of others once again very real.

It's the same feeling I had years ago when I met D.L. Langford.

If Gabby was at one extreme of the spectrum, resigned to accepting her unlucky fate and moving on, D.L. Langford was at the other.

Close to 90 years old, Langford was confined to a wheelchair and struggling to get by. He may have been elderly and infirm, but D.L. Langford was as informed as any investor.

The savings Langford counted on to get him through his final days had vanished under Jeff Guinn's watch. The monthly interest checks that had landed in Langford's mailbox each month had disappeared, replaced by letters from Guinn on Aspen letterhead. The missives on forbearance agreements and delayed foreclosure efforts held little hope for an elderly man like Langford.

D.L. Langford hailed from near the California farmland where Kenny Guinn grew up. Langford told me his sister, Clorie Gill, also an investor with Aspen, helped young Kenny financially when he was in school. It was a kindness Langford could not believe Guinn's son would forget now. But when the interest payments stopped and Langford, with the help of a young neighbor, made the trek from Northern California to Las Vegas to check on the status of his investments, he was unceremoniously booted from Aspen Financial's office, locked out and threatened with arrest for trespassing.

The Anointed Son

Jeff Guinn screamed at Langford, then hid in Aspen's offices, refusing to meet with the crippled, dying man who made the arduous twelve-hour trip by car to see for himself what was happening at Aspen Financial.

Langford was one of as many as 4000 investors, by Jeff Guinn's estimation, who entrusted their money to Guinn's Aspen Financial.[28]

All but a few who lost money attributed their bad fortune to the economy, never questioning Aspen's practices. The handful who dared to peer deeper would be vilified by the Guinn clan and its lawyers.

---

[28] Jeff Guinn deposition #1 p. 165

7: HIT LIST

When Jeff Guinn wanted something, he was a man obsessed. As a journalist, I was on the receiving end of frequent calls from Guinn when he was out to ruin a reputation or trying to generate regulatory scrutiny of a competitor. He was relentless. I would usually listen to hear if he had anything worthwhile, then half-listen as I turned at least some of my attention to something else. It was easier to humor Jeff Guinn than to hang up. After all, he was the governor's son.

I also know how relentless Jeff can be because I was the target of a Guinn-related vendetta. I was followed and my home was watched. A former cop, who was approached but declined to do the job, says my activity was reported to a Guinn friend and borrower, Susan Mardian, who apparently didn't enjoy the scrutiny my stories generated on her failed developments.

Lest I inflate my own importance, allow me to note: I was far from alone on Jeff Guinn's hit list. And I was far from the top.

In the early 2000s, Jeff Guinn's Enemy #1 was another hard money lender: a man named Mike Shustek.

If Jeff Guinn, by virtue of his father's position, was the consummate Nevada Insider, hard money lender Mike Shustek was The Outsider, a guy who came to Las Vegas to deal cards and likes to say he was homeless before he hit it big.

Shustek lacked the decades of dues-paying bona fides that Jeff Guinn inherited by virtue of his father, but he was willing to spend whatever it took to buy his way into the game, giving money to charities and using much of his own cash in an unsuccessful attempt to elect an Attorney General of his liking.

The Anointed Son

Though very different, Shustek and Guinn are, in many ways, cut from the same cloth. An attorney I know has deposed both. Their personalities, he says, are very similar. Both exhibit a friendly arrogance that cements a subtle certainty: each believes himself to be the smartest person in the room.

In the late 90s, Shustek's Del Mar Mortgage ran daily ads in the business section of the Las Vegas Review-Journal, offering double-digit investment returns. Later, under Vestin Mortgage, NFL great Joe Namath would serve as Shustek's spokesman until a famous sideline kiss cost Namath the gig.

Shustek quickly became a player in the hard money lending circle, brokering the loan that helped the Herbst family (owners of the Terrible Herbst gas station chain) build Terrible's Casino — a property that became the Silver Sevens following a Herbst bankruptcy.

Shustek's success did not go unnoticed by Jeff Guinn, who competed with Shustek's Del Mar Mortgage (later Vestin) for investors and borrowers, the respective heart and soul of the industry.

In 1997, two years after Aspen Financial opened, Shustek's company came under regulatory scrutiny when an anonymous letter to the state alleged wrongdoing. Shustek attributed the missive to a disgruntled employee who had gone to work for a competitor.

Perhaps coincidentally, Jennifer Hendricks, a former Shustek employee, had jumped ship to work for Jeff Guinn at Aspen Financial.

Just a month into Kenny Guinn's first term in 1999, the state briefly seized control of Del Mar Mortgage, and installed the governor's accountant, George Swarts, as receiver.

Both Swarts and the director of the state Financial Institutions Division, L. Scott Walshaw, say the timing of the Del Mar seizure was coincidental and not attributable to Guinn, though Walshaw admits Jeff Guinn was one of many hard money lenders who complained about Shustek's business practices.

"Jeff and others had voiced concerns, then ended up doing the same thing. All the hard money lenders were doing a version of the same thing. The loans were not based on ability to pay. And they weren't collateral lenders. The appraisals were based on the projected value of the property upon completion," Walshaw told me during a phone interview in 2015. His efforts to institute reforms during the Guinn administration fell flat.

Jeff Guinn's obsession with Shustek carried over into the next century. He would often call me with the names of disgruntled investors in Vestin Mortgage, the successor to Del Mar. The investors' complaints centered on whether Shustek was truly obtaining approvals from the required majority of lenders before taking action on loans.

Jeff hinted to me that Shustek was somehow manipulating the assignments of fractional interest in loans. It would have taken a title expert to unravel. I had neither an expert nor any evidence.

In March of 2003, Jeff Guinn was on his way to becoming one of the valley's biggest private lenders. He was keeping company with all the right players and, according to public records, had just purchased a home for $1.66 million in Belacere, a gated community near Peccole Ranch in Las Vegas.

Jeff Guinn may have had other competition in the hard money lending industry, but the governor's son had his sights on Mike Shustek's Vestin Mortgage.

8: THE REGULATORS

In June of 2003, the Las Vegas Review-Journal reported Governor Guinn refused to sign a bill that his son, Jeff, opposed. The measure created the Mortgage Lending Division, a provision Gov. Guinn's spokesman said the governor supported. But the measure also added regulation to mortgage bankers, which Jeff Guinn complained could cost his mortgage banking business as much as $50,000 a year.

The RJ story rehashed one of many high-profile failures that resulted in multimillion-dollar losses for investors. The story noted the revocation of Harley L. Harmon Mortgage Company's license for mishandling funds and misleading investors exposed flaws in the state's regulatory process.

At the time of the state's action, the Las Vegas company named after the former state assemblyman had handled $23.9 million from 694 investors. Much of that money was lost through phony deeds of trust. Harmon in February was found guilty of 34 counts of mail fraud in U.S. District Court.

The state also shouldered blame because it turned out that Harmon's company had produced questionable audit results, such as from sloppy record keeping, for several years before the state acted. ...

...Ironically, one businessman who could be adversely affected by the creation of a new division is Jeff Guinn, the governor's son. Jeff Guinn owns two local businesses, one that solicits investor money for construction loans and another that makes home mortgage loans.

He said he supported provisions of AB490 that will crack down on advertising spokesmen and give mortgage agents more options to take training courses in their field of specialty. But the inclusion of his home mortgage banking business irks him because he said it could increase his annual business costs by as much as $50,000 a year such as through added auditing expenses.

Another irony: a story in the Las Vegas Sun on AB 490, featured a quote from developer Howard Bulloch, who had won a $5 million judgment against Mike Shustek's Vestin Mortgage. Bulloch would go on to be one of Aspen Financial's largest default borrowers.

Bulloch, who blamed the Financial Institutions Division and its commissioner, L. Scott Walshaw, for being slow to address the developer's complaints against Vestin -- it took a court order to get the state to probe the company -- said he could see why the Legislature passed AB490.

"It's too bad the state has to pass new laws because the commissioner is not doing his job," Bulloch said. "This is an important issue that needs to be kept in front of the people because we do not need another Harley Harmon." -Las Vegas Sun, June 16, 2003

Guinn and his attorneys are quick to remind disgruntled investors, news reporters, attorneys, judges and anyone else who asks that Aspen Financial consistently received high marks from state auditors. The truth is the Mortgage Lending Division conducts examinations, while licensees such as Aspen are required to obtain their own audits. State examiners conduct routine checks of an extremely limited menu of items during their annual visits to Nevada's mortgage brokers. The Mortgage Lending Division was, by all indications, a failure at regulating the state's lending industry during the Guinn administration.

With millions invested in loans brokered by his son's company and monthly interest checks in the mail each month, Governor Guinn —at the helm of the state regulatory scheme —had every reason to look the other way.

In July 2006, the Reno Gazette Journal detailed yet another high-profile collapse in the hard money lending industry and revealed the failed effort to persuade Governor Guinn to augment staff during a time of unprecedented population growth.

In December 2003, the Securities and Exchange Commission obtained a federal court order freezing the $48 million in assets at Global Express. The SEC concluded that Global Express was running a "Ponzi-like investment scheme." Neither federal nor state charges have been *brought against (Connie) Farris. Understaffed after USA Capital filed for bankruptcy in April, state Mortgage Commissioner Scott Bice complained he had seven examiners available to review records of about 1,000 mortgage brokers, including those who help homeowners borrow from institutions and private lenders such as USA Capital. During the 2005 Nevada legislative session, Gov. Kenny Guinn limited requests for additional state positions to public safety and a few critical government functions, which did not include policing mortgage lenders, said Sydney Wickliffe, director of the Business and Industry Department, which includes the Mortgage Lending Division. Bice repeatedly asked the Legislature's Interim Finance Committee to authorize more examiners, Wickliffe said. But the committee said Bice should present the request to the full Legislature when it convenes in 2007.*

A December 2008 headline in the Nevada Appeal read: "Audit sharply criticizes Mortgage Lending Division."

The story said state auditors "found not only that 77 percent of annual examinations were not done in 2007 but that 87 percent of high-risk companies were not reviewed – 'The ones the public needs to be concerned about,'" said then State Assemblywoman Shelley Leslie. "The performance is abysmal and I don't know how anyone could say otherwise."

The story went on to say:

Auditors found the division failed to ensure that licensees submitted required financial documents including audited financial statements from high-risk licensees, didn't follow up on complaints, failed to collect some $490,000 in assessments owed in 2007 and 2008 and didn't collect administrative fines and settlement agreements totaling some $975,000. —Nevada Appeal, December 12, 2008

Aspen Financial was one of the "high-risk licensees" required to procure its own independent audit from time to time, a much different process than an audit by state regulators.

Jeff Guinn played all sides of the hard money transaction, acting as not only underwriter, broker, and servicer, but in some cases, borrower, too.

It's a practice called "Insider Lending."

In 2007, Jeff Guinn's Aspen Financial brokered (and earned a hefty loan origination fee) for a $19,550,000 loan to Jeff Guinn's Coronado Eastern LLC. On July 25, 2008, Coronado Eastern LLC notified Aspen's individual lenders that it could no longer make the full monthly interest payments on the loan, noting it had "approached Aspen with a proposal to address this loan" and went on to ask the lenders to accept reduced payments and forbearance on the remainder. A little more than two months later, Coronado Eastern notified Aspen lenders it could no longer make any payments and asked for their forbearance.

Outlawed in some states, insider lending has drawn scrutiny in Nevada, where the law requires investors be notified of the potential conflict of interest.

Legislative efforts to end the practice of insider lending fell short during Kenny Guinn's administration.

In 2008, Mortgage Lending Division Commissioner Joe Waltuch, appointed by Guinn's successor, Jim Gibbons, proposed changes that were written into law. Among them was a provision that insider loans constitute no more than 25 percent of a mortgage broker's outstanding loans or 100 percent of the broker's net worth.

According to public records, Jeff Guinn was a borrower on at least eight loans totaling more than $90 million, brokered by his own company — and all of them non-performing when the bottom fell out of the market.

9: TOP OF THE WORLD

Vicki Quinn and Monica Guinn lived less than a mile apart as the crow flies when the two met. Jeff and Monica Guinn lived in a gated community behind Our Lady of Las Vegas Catholic Church, where the Quinn and Guinn children attended school. Vicki Quinn testified in February 2013 about frequently seeing Jeff at the Guinn home when she'd visit during the day.

Q: (Dennis Prince): Did she (Monica) ever tell you how much time he was spending in the office? Like it was only an hour or two a day...?
A: She never said that to me, but I knew because he lived by my house and he was home all the time.
...He was always home. I'm like what the hell?

Q: Did that seem odd to you that he was always home?
A: Yeah
Q: Did you frequently go over to the house?
A: Always... I was there a lot I never-- I don't think I ever-- I don't think I was thinking it was unusual. I just thought they were doing well that, damn, you know, must be nice to be home all day. I mean, I didn't think that, you know, he was home because he was screwed up. I just thought he was home having -- because they were doing great. I mean to me they were on top of the world.[29]

Monica Guinn testified under oath in 2012 that in the year and a half leading up to Jeff's rehab, he never missed a day of work.

Q: You were mentioning yesterday that during Jeff Guinn's period of drug use prior to his rehabilitation that he never missed a day's work. Do you recall that testimony?
A: Yes.
Q: What kind of hours did he keep during that time period? And let's

---

[29]Victoria Quinn Deposition P. 109-110

limit it to say the year before he went into rehabilitation.
A: He showed up first thing in the morning, and stayed until probably 4:00 or 6:00 p.m.
Q: First thing in the morning?
A: Yes.
Q: 7:00 a.m., 8:00 a.m., 9:00 a.m.? What time?
A: He put in a full day's work.
Q: Eight hours?
A: Yeah.[30]

I personally know that Jeff was in the office in the mornings. Generally, when I called in the afternoon, he had left for the day.

---

[30] Monica Guinn depo p. 283

Chapter 10

10: Jeff "Quinn" Goes to Rehab

In June of 2005, Kenny Guinn was the governor of Nevada. His son, Jeff, was brokering hundreds of millions of dollars a year in commercial deals—the money loaned by and to some of the biggest names in town and some of Kenny Guinn's closest friends and campaign contributors.

With his money invested in dozens of Aspen loans (a face amount of more than $8 million that year, according to real estate records) and regulation of the hard money lending industry in his hands, Kenny Guinn had good cause to keep a lid on his son's addiction to prescription painkillers.

That is how Jeff Guinn came to spend his time in rehab under an assumed name.

Monica Guinn testified under oath in 2012 about her husband's effort to get clean, and how she enlisted the help of Steve Quinn, the man she claimed was enabling her husband's addiction.

Q: With regard to Jeff's rehabilitation, drug rehabilitation, who took him to the drug rehab facility?
A: I did and Steve Quinn did. ...
Q: Did Steve, did you call Steve for help?
A: Yes, he was there to help me.
Q: Did you call him for help?
A: I–yes. I don't, you know, I don't remember exactly how it played out. But yes, he came to help. ...
Q: And at that time, you considered Steve a friend of yours?
A: Yes.
Q: Obviously, close enough that you would confide in him, hey, we need to do something for Jeff and admit him to some sort of rehabilitation–

A: Yes, he was more than willing to help.

Q: Right. And you check into, did Jeff check in as Jeff Guinn or Jeff Quinn, Q-u-i-n-n?

A: Q-u-i-n-n.

Q: So you used Steve Quinn's last name.

A: Yes.

Q: Why did you do that?

A: For protection.

Q: From what?

A: So the media wouldn't get a hold of that. ...

Q: In 2005, was Kenny still the governor?

A: Yes.

Q: So why would you ask for help from Steve Quinn to admit Jeff into a rehabilitation facility if you thought that Steve was one of the problems? That he was partying with Jeff, giving him—they were participating in drug abuse?

A: I had no idea that they were partying together and the extent of their use together. I mean I knew they were. But I didn't know how bad it was. And to be honest with you, I was by myself trying to figure out how to help my husband. There aren't a lot of people you can turn to when your husband is going through—I don't know if you've ever witnessed someone coming off of taking Lortabs. It's not an easy situation to be in. Especially when you have small children.

Q: Okay, when you solicited the help of Steve Quinn, though, I mean obviously you felt that was someone you had trust and confidence in; right? At the time?

A: As much as you can.

Q: Right. And you obviously used his last name when you checked him into the facility. Then what was Steve doing that you felt was so bad and had such a negative influence on your husband?

A: What do you mean by that?

Q: Meaning why would you call Steve Quinn if you thought that he was part of your husband's problem? They were partying together and abusing drugs, why would you call him to help?

A: I didn't know the extent of what they were doing.

Q: Well, then why didn't you call his parents?
A: His parents weren't in town.
Q: Why didn't you call them and say, "Hey, we have a real problem with Jeff. Someone needs to get down here and help?"
A: They weren't in town. And he needed help immediately.
Q: Well, there must have been a problem in the weeks, months or years before this. So why didn't you call Dema and Kenny and say, "Hey, listen. Jeff is having a real problem. I need you to get down here and help me get him some help"?
A: I don't know. I guess maybe I should have called you, since you're going to dictate how I should have done it.
Q: Well, I'm not asking you to call me for anything, actually.
A: Well–
Q: I'm asking you–
A: -- you know what?
Q: --why you didn't call–
A: -- I'm not going to go back to 2005 and have you dictate on how I should have done things. This is how it happened. This is what was done. I did the best thing I could do for my husband. So you can go on to your next question.[31]

Despite her reluctance, Jeff Guinn's wife, Monica, ultimately revealed her husband's sometimes rocky relationship with his mother.

Q: Did you ever hear Jeff express to somebody he hated Dema?
A: Yes, he has said that. But he doesn't really mean it.
Q: Well, he said that over a period of years though. Right?
A: Yeah. But he didn't mean it.
Q: What about Jeff's relationship with his father? Did he have issues to work out also with him?
A: No. No, he loved his dad. ....[32]
Q: Did you ever ask the Quinns to accompany you and Jeff to dinner

---

[31] Monica Guinn P. 109 -111

[32] Monica Guinn p. 207

when Jeff's parents were present?
A: I think so.
Q: Did you ever tell them that you would not go to dinner with Kenny and Dema unless Stephen and Vicki were present?
A: I guess. I can't remember.
Q: Was there a problem with your relationship, did you and Jeff have a problem with the relationship with Kenny and Dema at some point in time that you needed the Quinns to be there?
A: I think it was strained for a little while. But that all got worked out.
Q: When did it get worked out?
A: Probably a little while after that.
Q: What was it strained over?
A: I think Jeff had things to work out with his mom.
Q: What sort of things?
A: Just they didn't always get along. But they've worked that all out. [33]

Vicki Quinn testified in 2013 that Jeff Guinn was swallowing more than 100 Lortabs a day when Monica Guinn sought the Quinns' help getting Jeff into rehab.

A: I recall Monica calling me in the afternoon, I want to say, 1:30 or 2 because their children weren't out of school yet. And she said Vicki please get over here. I need you, and, you know, Jeff is in bad shape. And I got up there, and Jeff was in really bad shape. It was very sad.
Q: And what did you do?
A: I called my husband because it was way out of my scope of what to do. And Jeff Guinn's in his big beautiful bed in their beautiful bedroom.
Q: And then he was taken to a rehab center?
A: That same day my husband and Monica took him.
Q: Who made the decision to take him?
A: Monica, immediately.
Q: Ok. And how long was he in the rehab center?

---

[33] Monica Guinn p. 206-207

A: ...I believe it was a 30-day program.[34]

Vicki Quinn went on to testify about Jeff Guinn's emotional state before rehab.

A: He would get very angry very fast. And he was very-- you know, very troubled. He didn't act appropriately a lot of the times and I think it was because of the pills.
Q: When you say "he didn't act appropriately," what do you mean by that?
A: Just, you know, the things he said to his children and, the way he treated his children, mainly his oldest son. I mean, he had some issues that were, you know, sad to me.
Q: Did he have trouble controlling his emotions, what you personally could observe during that period of time?
A: The few times I observed it, yeah.[35]

The Ruthes' attorney, Dennis Prince, asked Monica Guinn about her husband's relationship with their children and whether the Quinns witnessed any abuse of the Guinn children.

Q: Did any physical abuse of the Guinn children occur at the Quinn's residence in front of them?
MR. PRINCE: At the Quinn residence.
Q: At the Quinn residence.
A: Not that I recall. I know my husband, like I had said, will yell at my kids just like any parent yells.
Q: I remember that testimony.
A: Yeah.
Q: What about at your home, was there any physical abuse of the Guinn children while the Quinns were present?

---

[34] Vicki Quinn P 21-22
[35] Vicki Quinn p. 110

A: Again, not that I recall. It was the same, same thing.[36]

Allegations of child abuse would surface years later, at the most inopportune time for Jeff Guinn.

Donna Ruthe was not only an Aspen investor. The long-time realtor also worked on projects with Jeff Guinn until a falling out in 2007. Ruthe testified under oath about Guinn's drug use, after some objections from Guinn's attorney, Bruce Willoughby, who complained the testimony was designed more to embarrass Guinn than to elicit responses for use at trial.

Q: (BY MR. PRINCE) The last question was did Monica ever tell you that Mr. Guinn's drug abuse was affecting or impairing his judgment or ability to perform his work?
A: Yes. She was very concerned.
Q: What was she concerned about—
MR. WILLOUGHBY: Before you answer, I'm going to object. Speculation.
Q: (BY MR. PRINCE) Go ahead and answer.
A: She stated that she was very concerned with overseeing Aspen and the development and that he was relying too much on Kent Barry.
Q: Did he believe that the -- did Ms. Monica Guinn believe that Jeff had delegated almost all the authority and oversight of the construction projects to Kent Barry and this was in part caused by Jeff's dependency on narcotic pain medication or abuse of narcotic pain medication?
MR. WILLOUGHBY: Again, objection. Speculation. Vague and ambiguous.
Q: (BY MR. PRINCE) Go ahead and answer.
A: She indicated that.[37]

...

Q: Did Jeff ever admit to you that he had a drug problem? Did he acknowledge it to you ever?

---

[36] Monica Guinn p. 282-283
[37] Donna Ruthe deposition, 2008, Quinn v. Metro P. 80

The Anointed Son

A: Not during the period that—when he came out of the rehab.
Q: When he came out of rehab, did he acknowledge a problem?
A: Yes. Not right away. Later on. It might have been six months or almost a year later he admitted it. I already knew it from Monica that there was a problem. That he had had a problem.
Q: What did he say to, how did he describe his problem?
A: He called me in one day. But I already knew he was going to do that, because Monica called me to tell me, "Jeff is going to call you in and tell you about that he was in rehab when he went away." So I was kind of prepared for it. And I had to make believe that I was just hearing it for the first time.
And he said, 'The time that I was sick, that you thought I was having a breakdown, or stress, and I went away for 30 days?" And I said, "Yeah." He said, "Well, I was, you know, I was at a rehab here in town." And he just told me that he was taking drugs day and night. And that was why Monica drove most of the time, the car. He just went into detail about it. I didn't ask what he took really though.
Q: Did he offer what he took?
A: I knew the two things he said he took was Oxycontin and Lortabs. He named those two. And I guess there's different forms of them or whatever. He named those two.
Q: Did he tell you how he took them?
A: No. I assumed pills.
Q: Did he smoke them? Did he inject them, to your knowledge? Did he describe anything like that?
A: I think it was pills.
Q: Did he tell you how long he had the problem?
A: I don't think he did. Monica had told me that he had it for a long time. That she was going to leave him, off and on several times, she was going to leave him, and had threatened that she was going to divorce him. But that he had the problems on and off for years. And she said it actually went back to when he was in college was his original problems. He admitted to that, too.
Q: So he admitted he had a longstanding history of abusing some type of drugs?

A: Right. When he told me this story when he was in rehab, he was extremely angry at his parents because they would not, they never showed to visit him.
Q: How did that affect him? How did he describe how that affected him that his parents didn't show up to visit him in the rehab?
A: Well, he said that his mother was a cold b-i-t-c-h. And that she was the one that kind of controlled what Governor Guinn did, with going there. And she was more worried about what the public thought than visiting her son. And Monica was in the room when this was said to me.
Q: Where was this said to you?
A: In Jeff Guinn's office, on 7900 West Sahara.
Q: And he said to you that during his stay in rehab, because his mother was concerned about how the press may potentially react to it, that she was a cold b-i-t-c-h, and therefore did not go to visit him?
A: Correct.
Q: Did they sever ties after that?
A: They didn't talk for a long time. But Monica said, and Jeff, that it was Jeff's mother that didn't make the attempt to call or see the kids. They blamed other people rather than themselves.[38]

Dema Guinn, despite her many attributes, is no Florence Nightingale according to her daughter-in-law, Monica Guinn, who testified about her mother-in-law in a 2012 deposition.

Q: Did you let Kenny and Dema know that you're checking Jeff into the rehabilitation facility?
A: They knew exactly where he was.
Q: Why didn't they, why didn't Dema come down and help you, his mother?
A: Because that's not in her nature. That wasn't her comfort zone. Everybody has a gift, and that's not her gift.
Q: What do you mean? I don't understand what you mean by a gift.
A: That wasn't her comfort to go there.

---

[38] Ruthe P. 187-188

Q: I don't know what you mean by comfort. You're talking language I don't understand. You need to be more specific than that. ...
A: It wasn't comfortable for her to go see. She doesn't go see people in hospitals or in rehab facilities. Either one. ...[39]

While Dema Guinn was absent as her son prepared to enter rehab, Vicki Quinn was present, seemingly a surrogate for Jeff Guinn's mother. In deposition, Quinn recalled the scene in the Guinn home that day in 2005.

A: And I, as Monica was pacing around trying to figure out what to do with, their doctor who was there, Dr. Green, I just kind of curled up in bed with him (Jeff) and held him in my arms and just made sure to let him know he was going to be okay and stroked his arms, and pretty much felt sad.[40]

Here's how Monica Guinn recalled Vicki Quinn's role that evening:

Q: Was she there to console him or offer him any assurances or support in any way that you recall?
A: Oh, sure, she was there to comfort, absolutely.
Q: Was she hugging him that evening?
A: Oh, yeah. Yes.
Q: Did she sit with him on the bed?
A: Oh, yes.
Q: Did she embrace him?
A: Yes, she was there for comfort.
Q: Okay. The Quinns were supportive –
A: Yes.
Q: -- to your family that evening?
A: Yes. ...
Q: Did you ever state to Steve Quinn that he was a saint for helping you out that evening?

---

[39] Monica Guinn p. 112
[40] Vicki Quinn P. 22

A: I'm sure I did. You know, that was a difficult night. So anyone that helps you through that situation you're grateful for. [41]

It may well have been Steve Quinn's saintly behavior that evening that would land Quinn and his family on Jeff Guinn's Hit List.

---

[41] Monica Guinn p. 248

11: Who's Minding the Store?

How did Aspen Financial operate during Jeff Guinn's stay in rehab? The answer depends on who you ask.

Here's what Vicki Quinn said in her deposition under questioning by Jeff Guinn's attorney, Joseph Liebman:

Q: Now, when Jeff went into rehab, you're, obviously, in constant communication with Monica, correct?
A: For those 30 days, yes, everyday
Q: And did Monica at that time tell you that she was going in to the offices at Aspen and actually, quote/unquote, running the business?
A: Yes
Q: And what did she tell you she was doing during that period of time?
A: She was doing whatever it took to make sure the investors didn't know that Jeff went in rehab. And she was running the business and having --she told me that Sean Corrigan
-- she couldn't do it without Mr. Corrigan and without Jeff's dad.
Q: Kenny Guinn?
A: Yes. They were helping her.[42]
...when Jeff was in rehab, the governor was coming into the office and working with Monica to help her. You know, Monica, as smart as she is, had trouble running the company when Jeff was gone. So the governor would come in. And I just assumed if the governor was in the office, this is an assumption, he, obviously knew what was going on because he would come down and help her run the business when Jeff was in rehab.
Q: When you say "he knew it was going on," what are you referring to?
A: I'm referring to that he would see what the loans and everything

---

[42] Victoria Quinn p. 102

were because he was in there helping Monica.[43]
...And then when Mr. Guinn was in the rehab, of course, I was very supportive to Monica. I felt kind of bad for her because she was, you know, trying to run the business as well as their household.
And, you know, I tried to get her to go out and do things with me or go to lunch. And she was so devoted and so committed to the success of their business and Jeff getting well, that she just engulfed herself into making sure that everything stayed afloat because of the business and because of the love she had for her husband. It was a mess.[44]

Monica Guinn, in a 2012 deposition, denied that Kenny Guinn, while governor, helped run his son's state-regulated company during Jeff Guinn's stay in rehab.

Attorney Dennis Prince: Did you ever tell a third party that you don't know what you would have done without Kenny during this period of time, coming in and overseeing things? Did you ever tell any third party that?
Monica Guinn: Not that I recall. He only came in one time to the office.

Q: Okay, when was that?
A: In the middle of – probably two weeks in. He only came into the office once.
Q: Has he ever worked there to do anything?
A: No.
Q: How about when Jeff was in rehab, did you ever ask Kenny to come in and assist you, keeping track of the business, looking over the business?
A: No, I did not.
Q: Has Kenny every maintained an office at Aspen?
A: He had an office there, but he didn't use it. ...
Q: So once the 7900 West Sahara building was built, an office was put

---

[43] Victoria Quinn p. 84
[44] Victoria Quinn p. 22-23

there for Kenny?
A: Yeah, we put one there, but he never used it.
Q: Was he ever in the office?
A: No. He would just come in to say hello and be on his way.
Q: Did you ever ask – while Jeff was in rehab, who ran Aspen?[45]
...

A: There were about three days that he wasn't able to, going through detox. But Jeff basically ran the business. But the executives that were in the office ran the business. But other than that, he was able to run the business while he was in rehab. All the paperwork was able to go to rehab.
Q: How long was he in rehab for?
A: About three and a half weeks.
Q: Is that here in Las Vegas?
A: Yes.
Q: And during that period of time, did you ever contact Kenny and ask him to come in the office and just, you know, help assist with operations, making sure things are run appropriately, all the protocols were being followed?
A: No.[46]

Attorney Dennis Prince asked Vicki Quinn about Jeff Guinn's drug abuse, and whether he tried to hide it from investors.

Q: As it relates to the drug abuse, did Monica ever tell you how long she believed that the drug abuse had been ongoing before he finally went into rehab?
A: It was ongoing when I met him.
Q: So in 2000?
A: Yes
Q: How did you know that?

---

[45] Monica Guinn p. 70

[46] Monica Guinn Deposition volume 1 p. 71

A: Because we talked about it. Monica would discuss it with me. And then it escalated. It got worse.
Q: So it got worse in that five-year period of time?
A: Yes. Yes
Q: Progressively worse?
A: Yes
Q: And at the end, I mean, what did you learn--what was his prescription drug addiction? What did it entail?
A: She told me he was taking 110 Lortabs a day when he crashed.
Q: And when she said "he crashed" how did he crash?
A: He, I think, might have either ran out or decided to quit, and that's when I was there helping him try to get through it until we got him into rehab that day.
Q: Did she ever tell you that it was important to her and to Mr. Guinn and Aspen, for that matter, that the investors not learn about his addiction and admission into rehab?
A: Yes, she did.
Q: Why?
A: Because she was worried that he was managing so much money under the influence for a period of time that she was worried that if they found out, it would really suffer their company.[47]

Did Jeff Guinn's prescription drug addiction affect his ability to operate Aspen Financial?

In the weeks before Guinn sought help for his addiction, Aspen syndicated a series of inordinately risky loans.

On April 25, 2005, Guinn signed an agreement with a bank called AmTrust, in which he subordinated the rights of Aspen's second mortgage lenders, effectively eliminating their recourse in the event of a first mortgage default on a Christopher Homes loan.

On May 20, 2005, Guinn brokered a second position investor-backed

---

[47] Victoria Quinn p. 103-105

loan to complete the purchase of a property on Grand Teton in Las Vegas, a 100% financed transaction.

On May 5, 2005, Guinn syndicated a close to $18 million loan for borrower Susan Mardian secured by the doomed Milano Residences project. Guinn cashed out the borrower for $2 million, ostensibly in consideration of a $4 million trust deed Mardian placed on the property in the name of her company, Joshua Tree, before the refinance. Here's how Mardian explained it when asked in a deposition if she really invested $4 million in capital:

"It was a point of reference for money that I contributed to the project either in equity, cash, future cash, future equity to secure my position."[48]

Mardian would wait two weeks, then place another deed on the property in the name of her company, Joshua Tree—this one for $4.5 million. Weeks out of rehab, Guinn allowed Mardian to cash out $4 million more, with no evidence of any commensurate investment.

Here's how she explained that cash draw under oath:

"That was another point of reference for equity and/or cash that I personally had contributed/invested in Milano as a way of securing it."[49]

Mardian pocketed more than $7 million in cash back on Aspen loans secured by the failed Milano project. The investors on the final first and second deeds of trust, totaling close to $30 million, were not so lucky. Some accepted Mardian-owned land in Arizona in exchange for releasing their interest in the defaulted loans. Susan Mardian's "equity

---

[48] Susan Mardian deposition p. 45

[49] Susan Mardian deposition p. 47

draws" would eventually pique the attention of the FBI.

Coincidentally, Mardian, like Jeff Guinn, admits to her own problems with pain medication. In a website testimonial ad, she touts a device that helped ease arthritis pain. Pain medication, she says, landed her in the hospital. (See picture of ad in photo section)

12: LIFE'S A BEACH HOUSE

Jeff Guinn's month in rehab did little, if anything, to quell his voracious appetite for spending.

Vicki Quinn testified in 2013 about Guinn's post-rehab buying spree, including the purchase of a second beach house.

Vicki Quinn: They owned one, and then when Jeff got out rehab, he told Monica if she would stick it out with him and stay with him, he would buy her one right on the beach. So at the time they owned two, and I don't know if they sold the other one. It was a block off. It was a really cute, little house. Then they bought one for about $13.5 million right on the ocean, and it was a gift to Monica for being so good and nice to Jeff and standing by him because she really did.
...every time that he, you know, did something terrible, that he would buy her something to forget about it or he would buy her sister something to forget about it. That's how he did it.[50]

Vicki was off by a few million. Jeff Guinn would testify he purchased the second beach house for $7.2 million in 2006 and sold it in a short sale for about half that in 2012. Guinn said the home was encumbered with $6.5 million in loans.

---

[50] Victoria Quinn depo p. 97-98

13: LAND SWINDLE

Cheryl Rogers was too young in 1954 to remember the episode of her father's program that aired Sunday, March 14th.

The synopsis for "Land Swindle" that night read: "Roy breaks up a land racket after a local newspaper runs a story questioning a property sale."

Cheryl is the daughter of Roy Rogers, the cowboy music and film star who rode to fame alongside his wife, Dale Evans, known affectionately as "The Queen of the West."

Rogers, whose married name is Barnett, would be without the help of her famous father when, as an adult, she'd run up against Jeff Guinn.

Rogers-Barnett was born into Country-Western royalty and raised on simple, reliable truths.

 "We were always told land is the best thing since it's always there," Rogers-Barnett told me during a 2010 interview for a story we were running on *Face to Face with Jon Ralston*.

Rogers-Barnett says she was no stranger to investing in land when she came upon Aspen Financial, and the fact it was owned by the governor's son gave her an added sense of security. Rogers Barnett and her husband had investments in twenty loans with Aspen Financial. When we met, I asked her how many were non-performing.

"At the moment, virtually all of them," she said.

Rogers Barnett's faith in land investments would be sorely tested by her experience with Jeff Guinn.

The Anointed Son

14: THE BOX

I was not the least surprised when I first learned of trouble between the Quinns and the Guinns. It was sometime in 2006. I had expected the friendship to fizzle in a fashion I had seen before with the Quinns. But this was different.

Vicki and her son Stephen came to my house on a Sunday morning. Vicki wanted my colleague at the time, Jon Ralston, to hear the story, too. We ate breakfast on my patio as Vicki filled us in on what she characterized as Jeff Guinn's attempts to ruin her husband.

Vicki said Guinn had filed complaints with the Contractors Board against Steve, and now there was a lawsuit. She said Jeff had no real gripes and that it was retribution for Steve refusing to procure prescription drugs for Jeff after his release from rehab. And she said Jeff was mad at her for rebuffing his attempt to buy her son's season tickets in the disabled section at UNLV Runnin' Rebel games. I had no interest in a construction defect story, Jeff Guinn's drug problem, nor his perceived snub over basketball tickets.

Vicki recalled the 2006 conversation during her sworn testimony in the Ruthes' suit against Jeff in February 2013, under questioning by Jeff's attorney Joseph Liebman of Bailey and Kennedy.

Q: Do you recall ever speaking with Ms. Gentry about Mr. Guinn?
A: Yes.
Q: What do you recall about that?
A: As my friend, I spoke to Dana Gentry about Mr. Guinn, not as Dana Gentry the reporter. That's very important for you to understand.
Q: When was that?
A: That's when my husband's life was getting ruined at the Contractors Board. I called up Dana and talked about it. I actually met her for breakfast. And she pretty much told me there's absolutely nothing

you're going to be able to do when the governor, who is a great governor, so well liked and respected, controls the state. And you're basically -- can I say—fucked. So what was the question?

...

Q: And did Dana turn that into a story?
A: Not yet, no.
Q: Do you recall any other conversations with Dana Gentry about either Jeff Guinn or Aspen Financial?
A: Well, when I got that box, you know, the big box of it's all that stuff in it, I didn't understand -- I called up Dana, my friend, not my reporter, and I said, Dana, you're not going to believe this, but Jeff Guinn is, like, following my entire family. And she told me I was crazy, I was nuts, he would never do that.

So then I got the box, and I started reading things I didn't understand. And I knew Dana, being a reporter, being extremely smart, would understand what things meant so I called her and I read a line, and said, so and so was SCOPEd. And she goes, SCOPEd! And she just went, like, crazy. ... So Dana explained to me what a SCOPE was and how Jeff was using Metro to do this. And it was just -- it was mind boggling.[51]

Mind boggling, indeed.

It was a Sunday afternoon in September of 2008, about two years after Vicki first pitched the story about Steve's construction defect case with Jeff, which I had not given a second thought.

Calls with Vicki were long. She loved to talk. Suddenly she was reading names, social security numbers, and birthdates of people neither of us knew nor had ever heard of.

---

[51] Vicki Quinn p. 39-40

"What are you reading? Where did you get these names?" I asked.

"It's from the discovery in the lawsuit I told you about," Vicki replied. "Documents we got from the private investigator Jeff hired to follow us. Binders full of them. Something called SCOPE."

"SCOPE? From Metro?" I asked

It was an acronym for Shared Computer Operations for Protection and Enforcement, a database of personal information and criminal history.

"How would a private investigator get background records from Metro? And who are these people?"

"I don't know," she answered. "Now are you interested?"

Vicki was referring to that conversation we'd had back in 2006. I'd had no desire to look at a construction defect case back then. They were a dime a dozen. Even the fact that it involved the governor's son was not enough to pique my curiosity.

But this was different. The governor's son appeared to be obtaining confidential information from the police, while his dad was in office. Or was it because his dad was in office?

"What are the dates on the reports?" I asked Vicki. "What years?"

"2007, 2007, 2006, 2006..."

2006! Bingo. Kenny Guinn's term ended December 31, 2006. A story is born.

"Vicki, I have to get those reports. Can you make me copies?"

"Copies? Are you crazy? There are thousands of pages. Come over and take what you want. Just bring them back before Steve finds out I gave them to you."

"I'll be right over."

15: THE COMMUNITY BANK LOANS

By Jeff Guinn's own admission, Aspen Financial brokered as much as $400 million dollars a year in loans. But Guinn was no stranger to borrowing. Heavily.

Guinn and company took five loans totaling more than $40 million from Community Bank, which added to the mountain of bad debt that would eventually bury the bank.

In 2004, Community Bank loaned Jeff Guinn and his business associates $4.7 million for the West Sahara office building that housed Aspen Financial.

Guarantors on the loan, according to court documents: Monica Guinn, the Guinns' Del Mar Trust, businessman Mark Brown and wife at the time Michele Brown, the Jeffrey & Monica Guinn Family Trust, and the First Couple's blind trust—the Guinn Irrevocable Asset Management Trust 1999.

The FDIC, which ultimately took control and closed Community Bank, would eventually sell the West Sahara property at public auction on May 31, 2011 for $3,849,170. The balance owed after the sale: $1,399,415.

In late September of 2005, Community Bank of Nevada approved a $250,000 line of credit for Jeff Guinn.

In March of 2006, Community Bank increased a Guinn line of credit to $600,000. A month later, Community Bank approved a line of credit for Aspen in the amount of $3 million.

By year's end, Community Bank would loan Jeff Guinn another $5.68 million secured by a jet, a 1984 Bombardier Challenger 601-1A. Court records indicate Jeff Guinn stopped making payments on that loan in

January of 2009. The FDIC agreed to let Guinn sell the plane. Guinn still owed $5.9 million after the sale, according to court records.

Aspen Financial Services brokered and serviced loans on property in Nevada, primarily in Southern Nevada. Why did a Las Vegas-based company doing business in Las Vegas need a jet? Guinn refuses to say.

In November of 2007, Community Bank loaned Jeff Guinn and his partners Sean Corrigan and Kent Barry $29 million to develop a mixed-use retail and office project at Green Valley Parkway and Horizon Ridge in Henderson. The trio made their payments for a little more than a year, through February of 2009, according to federal court records.

By April of 2009, all the Community Bank loans, with the exception of the one secured by Aspen's office building and guaranteed by Kenny and Dema Guinn's trust, would be in default. The last would soon follow.

16: Hookers, terrorists, and drug dealers. Oh, My!

Steve Quinn knew Donna Ruthe on a professional level. They had worked together on projects for Jeff Guinn. Steve built the buildings and Donna sold them.

Eventually, Donna Ruthe received a summons to a deposition in the construction defect case Jeff Guinn filed against Steve Quinn. It took place in January of 2008. Ruthe revealed a tale beyond belief.

Here's how Steve Quinn, in his own deposition, recalled Ruthe's story.

Steve Quinn: We were sitting in the deposition. We had become aware of things that were going on that had us dumbfounded that things of this nature had been going on against the Quinn family.[52]
...
Joseph Liebman (attorney for Jeff Guinn): What specific things dumbfounded you?
A: That I had been followed for a year and a half by a private investigator. That accusations had been made that I was dealing drugs out of my office building. Accusations had been made that I was running a prostitution organization out of my office building. Accusations were made that I had Muslim contacts.[53]

Jeff Guinn, according to Ruthe, had not only been paying a private detective to follow the Quinns, but also had Metro police watching Quinn's office for drug trafficking and prostitution! All while Guinn's father was governor.

The question that remained: why?

My theory: the Quinns had sorted through too much of the First

---

[52] Steve Quinn January 2008 *P. 42*

[53] Steve Quinn January 2008 P. 43

Family's dirty laundry, Vicki loved to talk, and Jeff hoped to scare her into silence.

Here's what Vicki Quinn told Guinn's attorney Joseph Liebman during her deposition:

Q: And how was Mr. Guinn after he came out of rehab?
A: You know, I got to tell you, that's when he started being really mean to my husband with the contractor's board and that kind of stuff, and I didn't really see him much after that. ... I didn't see him much after rehab because he turned on my husband with the Contractors Board and tried to destroy my husband's life to the utmost of his potential.
Q: You mentioned, I think you had put it that, Jeff turned on your husband. Do you have any reason to believe or any reason as to why that would happen?
A: Well, I think -- I don't want to speculate the answer because that's not what a deposition is, but I believe in my heart that Jeff really didn't want to be surrounded with people anymore that knew the dark side of his life and he just basically went to destroy us to -- just to -- I don't know. He just went out to destroy our family. And you know, I'm emotionally traumatized by the following, and I will never probably be the same after that. So I really don't care what happens to Jeff Guinn ...
Q: And when you, as you put it, Mr. Guinn turned on your husband, did that, in effect, end your relationship with Mrs. Guinn?
A: It eventually did, but she really is something else because she stayed my friend even when she was following me, which was bizarre. I didn't know what -- when I found out that they were following us and I had neck surgery and she was bringing me pasta while she's got a private investigator after me.[54]

Steve Quinn is a patriotic guy, and in 2006, he was a member of Nellis Air Force Base's Support Team, a position that allowed him to rub elbows with military elite.

---

[54] Vicki Quinn p. 25

The Anointed Son

Donna Ruthe testified that Jeff Guinn enlisted her to warn a retired Air Force General and his wife, as well as developer Randy Black (whose wife was in Vicki's prayer group), to avoid the Quinn's home or risk getting caught up in a drug raid.

Donna Ruthe: The only comment that I ever passed was that Jeff had asked me to warn -- it's a general that retired here that Chuck and I know very well, General Ihde and his wife Sally. And he told me that I should warn them about going to Steve's house because I knew when they moved here -- I was in the process of selling them a home -- that they were going there. And he (Jeff) said, 'Well, if you were a friend, you would warn them. They may be there when they raid the house one day.'
Q: Who is going to raid?
A: When they raid Steve's house for drugs. And so the only thing I told Sally Ihde was that -- what Jeff asked me to tell her. I actually said, "Mr. Guinn thinks that this would be -- if I'm a friend, I need to tell you this. I don't know if it's true or not, but this is what's happening."
Q: And what did you specifically tell Ms. Ihde?
A: I told her that Mr. Guinn had someone following -- because she was in shock that anything —at the Quinns. And that there were people going from the office that looked like shady characters, that there might be drugs involved, that Mr. Guinn thought there were drugs involved, and that he had someone following them. And he wanted you -- me to share with you, being we were friends and the General had just retired, out of respect, that he was in the Air Force -- he said you should tell him to be careful going there.
Q: So did Jeff say that he wanted you to get that information to the General so they would not go over to the Quinn home?
A: Specifically, he wanted me to tell him. He specifically wanted me to share or Chuck to share with Randy Black, which we never did.
Q: When you say that Jeff wanted you to share with Randy Black, what specifically —
A: Everything that was going on. He said it's all legal. You can -- you or Chuck -- my husband is very friendly with Randy Black. And he said,

"You should warn him." Or the people out at the base, you know. He said, "Steve walks out at the Air Force Base." He said, "They should know who the real Steve is." He wanted me to share that he had embezzled, and he wanted me to share the drug issue. And I wasn't going to put myself in the middle of that situation. The only person I ever repeated anything, because it was so shocking and new at the time and I believed all of it, was Sally Ihde.
Q: What was the general's wife, Sally's response to you?
A: "Oh, God."
Q: What else did she say?
A: We honestly didn't talk about it after that. Because I told her I didn't want to get in the middle. 'I think this is going to get nasty in litigation,' I said. 'I felt obligated to warn you about that. We've known each other for years,' I said. And that was it. I later updated her when -- on my feelings when I found out a lot of different things that I didn't know when I said something, that maybe what I told her was not true.[55]

In 2006, the economy was showing signs of slowing and Jeff Guinn was churning $400 million a year in risky loans, but his focus much of the time was on Steve and Vicki Quinn.

---

[55] Donna Ruthe 2008 p. 106-108

17: Co-Opting the Cops

Jim Thomas is a former Las Vegas police officer turned private investigator. Jeff Guinn hired Thomas in July of 2006, while Guinn's father was still governor. Thomas testified he was hired to protect Jeff Guinn and his family from Steve Quinn.

The reports Thomas compiled for Guinn were voluminous. And they were damning. Not so much for Steve Quinn, who led a routine existence, but for Jeff Guinn, because they eventually led to Thomas' deposition, which revealed the tip of a particularly chilling iceberg: the extent to which Jeff Guinn was using the Las Vegas Metropolitan Police Department to do his personal bidding.

Steve Quinn's office complex consisted of four buildings—one occupied by Quinn. Here's an excerpt from a typical report from private investigator Thomas to Guinn, on the vehicles entering the driveway to the complex:

"Also observed this week was a vehicle belonging to Celestial Leigh Fried and to Jamal Fayeq Rashid. Fried is a stripper contributing to Quinn's sexually oriented contacts while Rashid is a three time convicted felon for Possession of Ephedrine and Manufacturing Methamphetamine, Telephone Fraud and Transporting a Controlled Substance all out of the State of California. Rashid's presence at Precision Construction, Inc. definitely adds to the belief that there is drug trafficking going on at that location. Rashid lists a birthplace of Fresno, CA but he is of obvious Arab descent. A second subject, Amir Shauib was also observed at Precision Construction, Inc. This subject is an alien from Pakistan. Therefore, it appears that we also have a Muslim connection to Stephen Quinn." -March 23, 2007

Quinn's attorney, Dennis Prince, questioned Thomas about that entry at his August 25, 2008 deposition.

Prince: What's the basis for that statement, that he (Quinn) has

sexually-oriented contacts?
A: There had been a number of prostitutes.
Q: How many?
A: I don't know. I would have to go through.
Q: How do you know they're prostitutes?
A: They had records for prostitution.
Q: How many of them?
A: I don't know.
Q: How do you know they had contact with Mr. Quinn?
A: I know that they were going in Mr. Quinn's business.
Q: How frequently?
A: Frequently.
Q: Did you call for law enforcement and say, "Hey, I think something is going on over here?"
A: Mr. Guinn did.
Q: He called law enforcement?
A: Yeah, there was a surveillance out there by Metro Narcotics for several days.
Q: When was that?
A: While we were doing our thing. One of my reports by Julie Rosenthal mentions that she was stopped by these people from Metro Narcotics.
Q: When did that start to take place?
A: It's in here. I don't know. I don't remember dates.
Q: Who gave Mr. Guinn the information he's now tipping off law enforcement and they're doing surveillance?
A: He was reading my report, and he, so he contacted Metro, and they did a surveillance.
Q: Let's assume for a minute that it was true, that Mr. Quinn has something to do with prostitutes at his business. How would that affect Jeff Guinn at all, for his safety and for his family, as you described it?
A: I have no idea.[56]

---

[56] -pg. 154-155 James P. Thomas, August 25, 2008 Precision Construction, Inc.,

The Anointed Son

The money Jeff Guinn was shelling out to his private investigator was substantial. Jim Thomas found no need to ask too many questions of his client.

et al. vs. Guinn, et al. Case No. A519586

18: Getting Personal

Why would Jeff Guinn, a man who seemingly had it all, invest an inordinate amount of time, energy, and money in his quest to ruin Steve Quinn? In 2008, Quinn's attorney, Dennis Prince, asked Donna Ruthe under oath about Guinn's motivation.

Ruthe's answer revealed that Monica Guinn suggested Ruthe commit perjury if deposed.

Donna Ruthe: In my opinion, I think it got extremely personal. I shared that with his wife, Monica, that it would be best for all parties to get these settled.
Q: What was Monica's response to that?
A: Well, in the beginning she was, you know, she wanted it to get settled. Because the concern was, I knew I was on a list, I was told, again, I didn't see it, but Mr. Guinn said I was on a list for my deposition. And when I sat with Monica one time and said to her, "What do you think is going to happen if I were asked questions pertaining to Jeff, or Kent, or when you asked Steve to follow Jeff, what do you think is going to happen?" And quote of what she said -- this is when I had a different opinion -- she said to me, "Well, that never happened." And I said to her, "What do you mean that never happened?" She goes, "Just forget it happened. You'll say it never happened." So my opinion was changing greatly.
Q: So my record is clear: You were having a meeting with Monica Guinn and discussing the lawsuit between Mr. Guinn and Mr. Quinn, and that your name had been put on some type of witness list and you may have to give a deposition at some point. And you asked her, "What am I going to do when I'm asked questions about statements you made to me about the relationship between Jeff and Kent, and you even asked Steve Quinn to have Jeff followed?" Is that what you were just describing?

The Anointed Son

A: Yes. It wasn't a formal meeting. I was in her office. We had many conversations in her office. So she would come across the hall to my office. And she would be upset. So it wasn't a formal meeting. We were just chatting. And this was a topic often.
Q: All right. In your view, based upon what she said, "You'll just say it never happened," did you think she was asking you to lie under oath?
A: Absolutely.
Q: What was your reaction to that?
A: I laughed at her and said, 'Do you think I'm not going to remember? You want me to say I don't remember?' And she said, 'That never happened. I'm never going to say anything. It never happened.'
Q: So she told you that if she's asked similar questions under oath, she would say it never happened?
A: Yes.
Q: And lie about it?
A: Yes.
Q: Did that make you feel uncomfortable?
A: Very much so.
Q: Did that start to change your view on the Guinns and what they're seeking to do with this lawsuit against Mr. Quinn?
A: Probably the last six or eight months before, my view is changing on seeing what was happening legally to other people. The tale that I would get, the feelings that I would get of wanting to destroy people. Comments here and there, and I couldn't say exactly, but wanting to destroy. And it was similar to Mr. Quinn to Mr. Donohoe.
Q: Did Mr. Guinn ever say he wanted to destroy Mr. Quinn?
A: I could say yes. Not only was he going to destroy him, he would run him out of the town.
Q: Why did he say he wanted to destroy him?
A: I don't know why he would say that. It was in conversation on everything that was happening legally. He would get upset. He would get angry. And he would make the comments.
Q: Did my name ever come up in conversation?
A: Yes.

Q: What did he say about me?
A: He said you were an idiot, incompetent, this was over your head, and you didn't have the staff that his attorney had. [57]

---

[57] Donna Ruthe deposition vol. 2 2008 p. 171-174

19: You've Got Mail

Between 2003 and March 30, 2007, Aspen Financial brokered a series of sixteen loans on a property at Coronado Center and Eastern Avenue owned by Jeff Guinn, Aspen President Sean Corrigan, and developer Kent Barry. Jeff Guinn's company earned more than $1.2 million in origination fees for lending to Jeff Guinn.

The final Coronado Eastern loans, personally guaranteed by Guinn, Corrigan, and Barry, refinanced previous loans also brokered by Aspen with a new first trust deed in the amount of $19.5 million and a second trust deed for $2.3 million.

The list of investors given to the lenders at the close of escrow indicated Aspen Financial had put up more than $4.5 million—almost a quarter of the funds—for the first mortgage, which gave other investor/lenders a great sense of security. What they did not know is that in the next three months, Aspen Financial would sell all but one percent of its interest in the loan to other investors.

Payments eventually stopped when the principal and interest payments could no longer be refinanced.

Both loans ultimately foreclosed. Jeff Guinn's Aspen Financial failed to pursue any of the personal guarantees provided by Jeff Guinn and partners.

A dispute over the Coronado Eastern property would ultimately prove costly to Guinn, sparking the end of the Guinn's business and personal relationships with the Ruthes and the beginning of what would prove to be the most aggressive of many legal assaults mounted against Guinn and Aspen Financial.

It was July of 2007. Jeff Guinn had listed the Coronado Eastern property for sale through Donna Ruthe, who discovered that Guinn's partner, Kent Barry, had listed the same property with a leasing agent.

Ruthe confronted Guinn. Their business relationship ended over a phone call and a series of emails, in which Ruthe disclosed that thanks to a warning a few weeks earlier from Aspen loan officer Tania Steffora, Ruthe and her husband were already questioning Aspen's underwriting practices, from the creditworthiness of the borrowers to what Steffora characterized as inflated appraisals.

Donna Ruthe told Jeff Guinn in an email that Steffora said Guinn was changing and becoming less concerned with the value of properties and the welfare of his investors, and more concerned with closing large loan amounts that generated hefty origination fees.

"…you were making bad choices with the loans you wanted to do. She said that it was different when you started Aspen and now all you were worried about was making the money and financing your projects with inflated values."

Here's part of Jeff Guinn's email in response, errors intact.

Sent: *Saturday, July 07, 2007 1:23 AM*
To: *Donna Ruthe*
Subject: *Re: You need to know this*

I have recieved your email, I must say I am taken back by the over value issue. All of our loans have indepentant appraisals. The appraisers we use are on all of the bank approved projects list. We got a $33 million loan committment from a bank in town on our canyons project. the bank told us its was low in value, that we had underestimated the rents. Its being appraised again to show the increase in value. Tania is not a lender, she sells these projects based on our underwriting and the independant appraisals. As for the Bulloch loan, he did get that one cash out about year ago. this new one was extended three months so sean and I can sit down and reduced the cash out a lot. Gary Days loan has equity in it and we have not refinaced it becuase we are making gary day pay out of his pocket the payment on monday.

Later that month, Guinn "reduced" the cash out to borrower on the

The Anointed Son

next Bulloch loan to $2 million. With the economy worsening and no means of refinancing the already bloated loan to include the payments, Bulloch was about to default.

Thanks to the blow up with Guinn, Donna and Chuck Ruthe avoided adding Bulloch's Desert Land loan to their portfolio of soon-to-fail investments.

20: CITY NATIONAL BANK

On July 9, 2007, two days after Donna Ruthe confronted Jeff Guinn about the quality of his loans, Guinn found himself on the other side of a lending transaction.

Jeff and Monica Guinn borrowed $250,000 from City National Bank, and Aspen Financial Services borrowed $750,000. A little more than a year later, those loans would go into default for nonpayment. City National Bank would sue in September of 2009.

Those defaults, coupled with other unpaid loans, would eventually sound the death knell for Aspen Financial.

21: Pie in the Sky

Howard Bulloch is best known as the would-be developer behind the observation wheel that never was.

Bulloch owns the land across the street from the Mandalay Bay on the Las Vegas Strip. He engaged in a race with Caesars Entertainment to build the first jumbo observation wheel on the Strip. Caesars won. The High Roller is flying high. Bulloch's SkyVue never got off the ground.

Bulloch stopped making monthly interest payments in 2008 to Aspen investors on a loan secured by a parcel near the planned observation wheel. He owes just shy of $30 million in principal and another $20 million in unpaid interest for a decade of defaulted payments on that loan.

Bulloch's Desert Land, LLC purchased the parcel in October 2001 for approximately $9,075,000, courtesy of a $10,400,000 million loan from Aspen Financial, which rolled payments for eighteen months into the loan.

A year and a half later, in 2003, when the interest reserves for the first loan ran out, Aspen funded a second trust deed for $1,500,000, recorded 3/29/02. The purpose of the transaction: essentially a loan to Bulloch to make his next round of payments.

On December 21, 2004, Aspen issued a new first trust deed in the amount of $13,300,000, which took out the previous loans and left another $1.4 million for payments. The loan appears to once again have been created for no purpose other than to service the debt on Bulloch's previous loans.

The fourth loan jumped to $20,000,000 and paid off the existing first of $13 million. It included interest reserves and, according to Jeff Guinn in a 2007 email to Donna Ruthe, it provided cash out for Bulloch.

Kenny Guinn, who was governor in December 2005 when that loan closed, had $1.3 million dollars invested through his "blind" trust, a vehicle set up when he became governor to avoid just the kind of potential conflict posed when investing in your son's hard money lending company.

The fifth and final loan, funded on July 27, 2007, was for $25,900,000. The loan summary noted cash out to the borrower, Howard Bulloch, in the amount of $2 million.

Bulloch's associates—we'll call them The FOBs (Friends of Bulloch)—invested some $3 million, about 11.5% of the total $25,900.000 loan.

Within months, the FOBs had bailed, replaced by unsuspecting new Aspen lenders.

Two possible explanations:

1. Bulloch's associates knew Bulloch was in financial peril and would be unable to shoulder the payments without the benefit of yet another refinance, which seemed unlikely, given the economic downturn. Land no longer held the investment appeal it had in years past.

2. Bulloch's associates never intended to stay in the loan, and invested just long enough for Aspen to fund the loan.

It wasn't long before Howard Bulloch's interest reserves ran out and he was unable to make the payments on his own.

Neither Jeff Guinn nor Aspen Financial had a dime invested in that loan. However, the governor, by then out of office, had $994,404 at close of escrow held through his trust. Three months later, Kenny Guinn's trust sold some of its interest. Eventually the investment would go bad, with the governor and Mrs. Guinn on the hook for $744,417.

Aspen investor Jim Zeller testified about the Desert Land loan during his deposition in the Ruthe case.

Zeller: So, you know, the borrower has nothing. Nothing invested. ...The appraisal went up from 9 million or whatever it was when he bought it to a purported $65 million now, and there's nothing that's happened out there to make that anywhere close to real.
Q: Have there ever been any improvements made to the property?
A: None that I can see.

Zeller had a theory as to what borrower Howard Bulloch did with the cash that went to him rather than the project.

Zeller: In fact, I have reason to believe he built his house over in Queensridge with money out of that loan.
Q: Out of your loan?
A: Yes.
Q: Okay. So -
A: And the previous loans. I'm not saying it all came out of my loan.
Q: Did some money get distributed to the borrower out of your loan on Desert Land to your knowledge?
A: That's my understanding. I didn't know it at the time.
Q: So I guess that your point is if money out of those loan proceeds went to Mr. Bullock (sp) and he used the money to build his own house in part, then obviously --
A: Instead of improving the property that the loan was made on.
Q: Why do you have reason to believe that?
A: Just some investigations on what's happened on his house. And I've checked the county indices. There's no loans on it. The house is -- I don't know. Seven, eight, nine million. Who knows.[58]

Howard Bulloch did not return my calls requesting an interview.

---

[58] Jim Zeller deposition p. 36

In 2016, Jeff Guinn called a friend of mine and said he was getting back in the lending business and wanted to know if my friend would be interested in taking 25 cents on the dollar for money she's owed after almost a decade of no payments on the Desert Land deal.
Guinn said his mother, who still had close to three-quarters of a million dollars tied up in the loan, took the deal. When my friend declined, Guinn called back and sweetened the pot. I'm sure Guinn's mother will be happy to learn she could have held out for more money.

Today, Howard Bulloch is being sued by some of those Aspen investors who didn't bite when Guinn called offering pennies on the dollar.

In March 2018, Judge Elizabeth Gonzalez approved a "modification" that would have Bulloch pay the investors about fifty cents on the dollar to sign over their shares, giving Bulloch title to the property.

22: Daddy's Boy

While Kenny Guinn downplayed the trappings of being governor, his son Jeff reveled in his newfound power. Did Jeff Guinn use the aura of his father's position to get his way?

Dennis Prince asked Donna Ruthe back in 2008 when Steve Quinn was suing Guinn for defamation.

Q: Was Jeff the type of guy during your relationship with him that tried to use his father's governorship to his advantage and was boastful about that and tried to use his name and authority to get things he wanted done or accomplished?
A: He did a few things that—yes. I would say yes to that.
Q: Give me the examples that you're aware of.
A: When the problem happened at the contractor's board, when there was the whole issue —I think it's Gary Wells if I'm not mistaken
Q: Guy Wells.
A: Guy Wells. And Jeff placed a call to Terry Wright of Nevada Title because he wanted him to place a call to Spiro—I'm not—I think it's Spiro.
Q: Spiro Don Filios.
A: Yes. He's on the board.
Q: Correct.
A: The contractor's board. Because he was very upset. He was trying everything to get Guy Wells removed from the hearing. Because originally at the hearing I happened to go—Jeff had asked me to go that day, and they had asked if anybody objects. And I know Jeff was sitting there and Kent was sitting right next to me, and no one objected. And Jeff's attorney was there, and he didn't object. But after the fact, he then wanted him removed, so he placed some phone calls to different people. And he told me that Terry Wright called him back and that he tried talking to Spiros. And that they did not understand why the

problem was, but that they didn't feel comfortable removing Guy.
Q: Okay. So according to Jeff's comments, he contacted Terry Wright, who was president of Nevada Title–
A: Right.
Q: –for him to place a call to someone at the Contractor's Board–
A: Correct.
Q: –under the pretext that 'Hey, you know, Jeff Guinn has asked me to call you?' So like to create a buffer between him and the actual board member?
A: That's what he said, yes.
Q: Why didn't he call himself? Because he didn't want to have it look like an impropriety since his dad was the head of the contractor's board?
A: I'm not sure. What he did say was, you know, 'A lot of these guys my dad placed in the position.'[59]

---

[59] Donna Ruthe, 2008, p. 129

23: YOU SCRATCH OUR BACK…

Like many other community banks in America, Community Bank of Las Vegas found itself besieged by a portfolio of bad loans as the Great Recession approached. Among them, a $31,634,000 debt owed by McCormick Investments for the Astoria project, described in court documents as "a high density residential and commercial development, located at Fort Apache Road and Warm Springs Road in Las Vegas Nevada."

In 2009, legal pleadings written by Jeff Guinn's attorneys at the Bailey Kennedy law firm reveal Guinn helped pave the way for Community Bank to lend a troubled borrower more money in order to make its payment.

The lawsuit filed against the bank by Guinn and his partners Kent Barry and Sean Corrigan details a meeting held on March 5, 2008 between Community Bank executive Larry Scott and Guinn et al.

"…Mr. Scott informed Mr. Guinn and Mr. Corrigan that McCormick Investments, LLC could not make its interest payment on the $31,634,000 loan the Bank made to it. … Aspen was the beneficiary of a second deed of trust on the Astoria Project, which secured a $4,000,000 loan from Aspen to McCormick Investments, LLC.

Mr. Scott asked Mr. Guinn and Mr. Corrigan if Aspen would agree to allow the Bank to add an additional $1,000,000 to its first deed of trust in order for the Astoria Project's loan to stay current, while McCormick Investments, LLC attempted to secure other financing to pay off both Aspen and the Bank's loans. This would require Aspen to subordinate its $4,000,000 deed of trust to the Bank's $1,000,000 advance. Mr. Scott stated that he made this request so that the Bank would not have to report the Astoria Project loan as delinquent on its 10Q filing.

Mr. Guinn and Mr. Corrigan agreed to take the Bank's request for subordination to their lenders and requested a letter of intent from McCormick Investments, LLC regarding the new financing which would pay off both Aspen and the Bank's loans. ... The matter was put to a vote and Aspen consented to the subordination agreement on the Astoria Project."

In its complaint against Community Bank, Guinn and Aspen insinuate the arrangement obligated the bank to acquiesce to Guinn's demands because the bank

"...received a greater economic benefit from its relationship with Plaintiffs (Guinn) than with a typical arms-length lender-borrower relationship when it tied all the loans together and requested and received assistance with the Astoria Project in order to relieve itself from the loss of a non-performing asset and the concurrent obligation to report the Astoria Project loan as delinquent on its 10Q filing."

In other words, "We helped you deceive the Feds. Now, help us."

Subtle.

24: METRO IN HIS POCKET

In September of 2008, I got a call from an excellent source who told me he knew the name of the cop at Metro who was doing Jeff Guinn's dirty work, via Guinn's hired private investigator, Jim Thomas.

Sgt. Paul Osuch was alleged to be coughing up private information on individuals who did nothing more than drive into the parking lot of Steve Quinn's office building. The source said I could use the name, but not where I got it.

"You're certain on the name?" I inquired of my source. "The last thing I want to do is finger this guy and be wrong. Not only for him, but for me. Metro will close the investigation and never take another look if I give them a wrong name."

"Yes, I'm sure," my source replied.

My source was impeccable. Still, I was hesitant to use the name.

Jon Ralston suggested I get Metro's policy and procedures on SCOPE violations, which I did.

A single offense was punishable. More offenses were grounds for termination. Hundreds? I wondered what that would get you. A public flogging? As it turned out, not much.

It was mid-September when I contacted Metro. Although I had the name of the prolific Paul Osuch, I didn't want to identify him. Could one person pull all those SCOPES? I had suspicions someone else could be working with Guinn's PI. I didn't want Metro to look at just one cop.

I put in a call to a Metro spokesperson, who said he'd look into it and call me back.

Instead, I got a call back from Captain Jim Owens.

It's never easy to inform anyone of potential wrongdoing by one of their own, especially cops. And although I am frequently at odds with police, I have the utmost respect for honest cops who put their lives on the line.

I was shaking, my voice quivering when I told Captain Owens of my suspicions, that someone in the department was leaking confidential SCOPE information, maybe hundreds of reports, to a private investigator who was working for the governor's son.

I could tell from the silence that he was completely dismissive of what I had just said.

"And just what ax do you have to grind against the police?" he asked.

The nerves that had plagued me a few seconds earlier evaporated, replaced by anger.

Like any seasoned journalist, I'm used to attempts to kill the messenger. But that doesn't make it easier to shrug off.

Against my self-imposed vow to keep the name to myself, I decided to give Owens a roadmap.

"Check Sgt. Paul Osuch's computer!" I blurted out. "And call me back."

The call from a contrite Captain Owens came a few weeks later.

"You were right," he said.

"How many did you find?" I asked.

"They are still counting. But we found enough to sustain a complaint," he replied. "We are still looking at other computers."

"So, these were all on Osuch's computer?" I asked.

The Anointed Son

"I'll let you know if there are others."

"What will happen to Osuch?" I inquired. *I hate costing anyone their job,* I thought to myself.

"He's taking early retirement," Owens responded.

What? A cop repeatedly violates department policy and gets no punishment?

"He won't get his retirement badge."

Retirement badge? Who cares? I would later learn that badge conveys significant perks for retired cops, enabling them to also carry their service weapon, but at the time it seemed a miniscule punishment for a major infraction.

My attempts to reach Paul Osuch for comment failed.

Years later, the target of Jim Thomas' investigative efforts on Guinn's behalf, Steve Quinn, would meet Osuch at a legal proceeding involving a federal lawsuit that Quinn filed against Metro. Quinn told me the two hit it off, and described Osuch as "a really nice guy."

25: WRIGHT GUY IN THE RIGHT PLACE

Jeff Guinn's Aspen Financial Services was a cash cow for Nevada Title, one of the state's largest title and escrow companies, which earned thousands of dollars each time Guinn refinanced a loan.

And when Guinn needed a favor, Nevada Title appeared willing to oblige.

Donna Ruthe testified in 2008 that when Guinn was out to ruin Steve Quinn and wanted to know if Quinn could pay the $1.3 million Guinn anticipated collecting on his unproved claim that Quinn stole from him, Guinn turned to Nevada Title for Quinn's financials.

Dennis Prince: At some point did Mr. Guinn ever—that's -- did he ever show you any personal financial records from Mr. Quinn?
Donna Ruthe: Yes.
Q: What did he show you?
A: He had a financial -- that's when he made the statement that he didn't have the money to pay off that 1.3. He had some financials from some job or something that Steve had to give someone at Nevada Title about it for him. And I think he said he asked Robbie Graham at Nevada Title, and she supplied him.
Q: Who is Robbie Graham at Nevada Title? Who is that?
A: I'm not sure if her title is president or what she is of Nevada Title. She works under Terry—for Terry Wright. I'm not sure of her position there.
Q: Okay. Did he say he called Robbie Graham about Steve Quinn?
A: That's what he told me.
Q: And what did he call her for?
A: He wanted a copy of the file he asked her for of something. I think Steve closed a building or some land on Western that he developed, and he wanted all the information on it.

Q: What information was he looking for? Did he say to you?
A: I don't know. As I said, when I went in and we got into these things, I wanted to get out of the office.[60]

Robbie Graham and Nevada Title declined comment.

Terry Wright is the longtime owner of Nevada Title, and was a longtime friend of Kenny Guinn. The two served together on a variety of boards. In April of 2008, Jeff and Monica Guinn sold their house in Belacere, purchased a few years earlier for $1.4 million, to Wright and his wife, Dana for $2.7 million—a hefty profit, given the collapse of the market.

The Guinns constructed a home next door, which they later sold in a short sale.

Within a few months, Wright transferred ownership of the Guinn's former house to Nevada Title, a move his employees testified they'd never seen before.

Under deposition, Wright said he bought the home because his wife liked it, but because of marital troubles, they never moved in. Nevada Title eventually sold the property.

Here's what Nevada Title executive Troy Lockhead said under oath about the transaction years later:

Q: Is Nevada Title Company in the business of owning residential property?
A: No.
Q: Have you ever seen Nevada Title Company your 23 years buy residential property and put it its own name?
A: No.
Q: Did you ask anybody why Mr. Wright was transferring the property to Nevada Title Company?

---

[60] Donna Ruthe, 2008 deposition p. 143

A: No. [61]

Terry Wright has declined to be interviewed regarding the transaction.

---

[61] Troy Lockhead deposition p. 127

26: ALL THE KING'S HORSES

Some say the recession was the best thing that ever happened to Jeff Guinn and Aspen Financial, because it gave Guinn an out, a scapegoat. Most investors licked their wounds and walked away, cursing their own bad luck.

But when the checks stopped coming and Jeff Guinn blamed the economy, not everyone was buying Aspen's explanation. The boom, they said, may have concealed Aspen's scheme, but the bust exposed it.

The already crumbling walls at Aspen Financial began to come down in November of 2008 when a group of investors filed what would become the first of many lawsuits.

Among the plaintiffs were longtime title and escrow executive Jim Zeller and retired attorney Charles Thompson, who alleged, among other things, that Jeff Guinn engaged in self-dealing, acting in his own best interest before investors', and failing to disclose it.

Jeff Guinn, who had become as experienced at borrowing as he was at lending, was having trouble keeping his head above water. He and his wife had defaulted a month earlier on a $250,000 loan from City National Bank, and Aspen was in default on a $750,000 loan from the same bank.

But it was Guinn's co-opting of Metropolitan Police that made news for the first time the night of November 20, 2008 on the television program I produced, *Face to Face with Jon Ralston*.

27: "I THINK HIS NAME WAS KAI."

I had waited months to meet and interview Donna Ruthe, having heard from Vicki Quinn that Ruthe had a wealth of information about Jeff and possibly knew the name of the Metro Police detective allegedly in Jeff's pocket.

It took forever for the Quinns to agree to give me Ruthe's number. Vicki had described her as a fiery Italian. I found Donna Ruthe to be professional, her words carefully chosen and measured, her memories clear and vivid. It was late November 2008. We were still in a sweeps rating period. My story on the Osuch caper at Metro was ready to go. All I needed was some sound. Mrs. Ruthe did not disappoint.

The program began with Jon Ralston's voice-over and pictures of police followed by a shot of Jeff Guinn.

"How would you feel if Metro Police released your confidential information? A lawsuit involving a prominent Las Vegan reveals a disturbing use of public agencies for harassment and private gain. And, your identity could be at risk. How could the police, charged with preventing identity theft, potentially be perpetrating it? Face to Face investigates."

My recorded story showed a shot of Jim Thomas' deposition, who testified that while he was conducting surveillance for Jeff Guinn, Guinn, without his knowledge, contacted the police directly.

Thomas: ... he took it upon himself to call the police department. I didn't know about it until after he did it.
Q: What did he tell you?
Thomas: That he called the police department, and Metro Narcotics

was going to do a surveillance. [62]

Donna Ruthe said in our taped interview that Jeff had a detective at Metro in his pocket.

"He would call someone, even in front of me. And I think the name was… he told me it was a detective on Vice… and I think his name was Kai. And he would call him to follow, to check out the Quinns, to put police officers in front of the house to see what was going on and just to run things for him."

I went on to note I found no evidence that Kenny Guinn was involved in procuring information from the police, but I did suggest the fact that Jeff was the governor's son may have swayed the cops to do his bidding.

On the same day Donna Ruthe appeared on Face to Face, Jeff Guinn's attorney sent letters to Dennis Prince, Steve Quinn's attorney at the time, threatening to sue him for "violating a court order" and disseminating defamatory statements and documents. Donna Ruthe got the same letter.

I don't know how testimony contained in a deposition could be defamatory, since it is protected by litigation privilege.

Dennis Prince said as much in his missive back to Bailey.

"All statements, even if any statements that we may have made, whether false or not, would always be absolutely protected by the litigation privilege," Prince wrote.

The litigation privilege: the equivalent of a free pass to lie in court. It was a privilege Bailey would soon employ in what I surmise was his

---

[62] P. 158 August 25, 2008 Jim Thomas deposition

Chapter 28

effort to stop my reporting.

For the record, Prince also noted he had not given me the deposition, but that it had been attached to a legal motion, filed as a public record at the court house.

In late December, Assistant Sheriff Ray Flynn confirmed that Paul Osuch retired before Metro Police could take any disciplinary action. The investigation turned up three or four SCOPEs run by Osuch and 227 DMV checks, which included sixty-six SCOPE reports. It also revealed an investigator in the Public Defender's office ran 248 SCOPEs for Jeff Guinn, including one on his son's roommate. The search of the investigator's computer, according to a well-placed source, turned up something else: material wholly unsuitable for the office. The investigator turned up unemployed.

The unanswered questions remained: why did Metro Internal Affairs wait from October 7, 2008, when it received the complaint, until after my story aired in late November to interview Osuch? I assumed the police simply did not want to know the truth.

And who was the detective Jeff boasted of having in his pocket? What had Donna Ruthe called him? *Kai.*

"How many Kais do you have in Metro?" I asked Assistant Sheriff Flynn.

"Two," he replied. "One in Internal Affairs and one on patrol. None in Vice. Dana, face it. We may never know who Kai is."

28: Citizen Guinn

Kenny and Dema Guinn purchased their Las Vegas home on Campbell Circle in 1974.

But 35 years later, in 2009, Kenny Guinn filed a homestead exemption on the residence, an action generally taken to exempt property from being seized in a legal judgment.

In February of 2009, Kenny Guinn was no longer governor. But he was acting as a statesman, trying to negotiate a solution to his son's accumulated debt with Community Bank of Nevada, totaling more than $40 million.

With a cross-default provision in place, Kenny Guinn, who was also a guarantor on at least one loan, had an interest in maintaining all in good standing.

Kenny Guinn's financial disclosures while governor make no mention of the debt owed to Community Bank nor his interest in Coronado Aspen II LLC, the landlord for Aspen Financial. But at the dawn of the New Year, the Guinn family's debt to the bank appears to have weighed heavily on the former governor's mind.

Jeff Guinn, Kent Barry, and Sean Corrigan asked for a twelve-month extension on one loan and requested Community Bank fund the tenant improvement loan that Guinn, Barry, and Corrigan claimed the bank had already agreed to fund. The bank balked, even with the master negotiator, Kenny Guinn, at the bargaining table.

The next step for Guinn and Company was a lawsuit claiming Community Bank reneged on an alleged promise to fund that tenant improvement loan.

"The Bank's deliberate intertwining of the loans at issue were designed to ensure that Plaintiffs—each and every Borrower and Guarantor—bear the burden of the performance or non-performance of every loan, and therefore creating a special relationship between the Bank and all Plaintiffs."[63]

Community Bank's response to the suit was simple. To paraphrase: pay us the money you owe on other defaulted loans and we'll talk.

In August of 2009, the FDIC closed Community Bank and seized control of the assets.

The Las Vegas Review-Journal reported the failed bank's financial condition:

Community Bank of Nevada reported capital of about five cents for every $100 of assets in its June financial report, while most banks have $10 of capital or more for each $100 in assets. Nonperforming assets, which include delinquent loans and repossessed real estate, were 30 percent of total loans on June 30.

...

The banking company last October reported a $3 million loss, down from $4.6 million in the second quarter. Jamison counted 13 loans for $147 million that comprised 80 percent of the banking company's nonperforming loans. -LVRJ

What that story in the Las Vegas Review Journal failed to mention was that the former governor of Nevada, his son, and his partners played a considerable role in the bank's downfall.

The fallout from the Community Bank episode rippled not only through Southern Nevada, but across the state line into Arizona, too.

A federal lawsuit filed July 13 in Phoenix accuses Edward Jamison of Las Vegas, CEO of the parent company of both banks, and other executives of negligence and breach of fiduciary duty for allegedly failing to

---

[63] Guinn v. Community Bank July 2009

manage Community Bank of Arizona in a sound manner.

The suit says the parent company, Community Bancorp Inc. of Las Vegas, purchased Community Bank of Arizona in 2006 and that almost immediately Jamison caused the Arizona bank to increase its concentration in risky commercial real estate loans.

Many of these loans involved developments in the Las Vegas area, and Jamison's strategy involved transferring risky loans from Community Bank of Nevada to Community Bank of Arizona, the lawsuit said.

These risky loans harmed the Arizona subsidiary as 75 percent of the loan participations it purchased from Community Bank of Nevada became problem loans for the Arizona bank at the time of its failure, the lawsuit said.

The suit said Jamison's justification for moving the loans from the Nevada bank to the Arizona bank was to reduce the Nevada bank's high concentration of commercial real estate loans while producing additional revenue for the Arizona bank. [64]

Legal documents filed in federal court note the FDIC, acting as receiver for the failed bank, sold the Coronado Canyons property at Horizon Ridge and Green Valley Parkway at auction for $3.7 million in April of 2011. The amount Guinn and Company owed Community Bank at the time, according to court documents: $32,601,000.

---

[64] Vegas Inc, July 23, 2012

29: SHERIFF CHAGRINED

In early March of 2009, Sheriff Doug Gillespie appeared on *Face to Face* and promised a new day at Metro. He confirmed a "ridiculous" number of SCOPEs had been run on Steve Quinn, his family, a handful of acquaintances, and mostly unfortunate motorists who ventured into a driveway near Quinn's building. Gillespie said the internal investigation was ongoing.

Little did the sheriff know that Metro would soon be forced to launch a second internal probe to investigate the first.

30: NO INVESTIGATION WARRANTED

Charles Thompson was a curmudgeonly sort.

I once walked out of an interview with him at Starbucks when he pointed a straw at me and yelled that I'd better get on board with Aspen's detractors. As my eyes welled up with tears, I stammered that I don't get "on board" with anyone, and I walked out. I didn't speak to him for months.

In 2009, Thompson was busy compiling briefings for regulators, state and federal, who might take an interest in Aspen. In March, Thompson heard back from the woman in charge of the State Department of Business and Industry, the agency that oversaw the Mortgage Lending Division.

Dianne Cornwall wrote to Thompson that "nothing you sent to me would warrant opening an investigation into the mortgage company in question. ...I also explained to you that I had forwarded the information to my Deputy Attorney General for review just to ensure that I was not missing anything that might warrant an investigation. The Deputy Attorney General agreed with me, i.e., nothing in the materials you provided to me would warrant the initiation of an audit/investigation."

Nevada vests in its Attorney General the power to take action against mortgage brokers. I heard from Nevada AG Catherine Cortez Masto the day my interview with Dianne Cornwall aired on Channel 3, the NBC affiliate, in Las Vegas.

Masto said she knew nothing of her office's review of the complaint and promised to look into it.

I never heard back from Cortez Masto regarding Dianne Cornwall's letter stating Aspen Financial warranted no investigation.

Nor did her office take any action when I reported in 2013 that Guinn testified under oath that he routinely broke the state's mortgage law regarding disclosure, and audaciously claimed he had the OK from regulators to do so.

The standard line from the Attorney General's office was that the disputes between Aspen Financial and its investors were a civil matter. Regulators, who claimed to be overburdened with fallout from the mortgage meltdown and enduring staff reductions because of recession-related budget cuts, were all too happy to defer the tough cases to civil judges and juries.

The problem: few citizens have the resources to mount a costly legal battle, which is one reason we have regulators in the first place.

31: IN SEVEN MILLION

In April of 2009, Chuck and Donna Ruthe joined a growing list of disgruntled Aspen lenders who were lining up to take Jeff Guinn to court. The monthly interest payments, which had previously come like clockwork, had dried up since the recession, lenders were getting antsy about falling property values, and Aspen, unlike many other hard money lenders, appeared to be in no hurry to foreclose or enforce personal guarantees.

The Ruthes' suit alleged Guinn failed to fulfill his fiduciary obligation to investors and refused them access to other investors as well as information regarding impounded construction funds at Nevada Construction Services, a company owned by Nevada Title owner Terry Wright.

The suit alleged that Aspen had misappropriated money, using proceeds from one loan to make payments on another.

Donna Ruthe reluctantly talked about the extent of her and Chuck Ruthe's investments in Aspen Financial in a 2008 deposition in Steve Quinn's case against Jeff Guinn.

A: There's probably at this point -I would say probably around seven million.
Q: What was it in July of 2007?
A: Probably –
Q: Just your best estimate.
A: I would say maybe 15. 12 to 15.
Q: 12 to 15 million?
A: Yes.[65]

---

[65] Donna Ruthe 2008 deposition p. 36

Parkinson's Disease was taking its toll on Chuck Ruthe. He wanted to go on the record before it was too late. During a taped interview for *Face to Face* in April of 2009, Ruthe suggested Jeff Guinn belonged behind bars.

"I thought there was fraud involved," Chuck Ruthe told Ralston.

"What made you say that? That's a serious allegation," Ralston asked.

"I believe that there is fraud involved with Jeff Guinn."

"Tell me why you believe that?"

"Whether you've invested $5000 or millions, it affects you the same way, and I think everyone is the same way."

Ralston asked Chuck Ruthe, "This can't be just about money to you... what is this really about?"

Chuck Ruthe answered, "Jeff committed fraud, he's going to have to pay for it some way."

"What would satisfy you?"

Ruthe replied, "Well, in my opinion, he'd go to jail."

"Really, it's that serious?"

"Yes," Ruthe answered.

"How many people do you think were defrauded in these kinds of transactions?" Ralston asked.

"Hundreds... some were only $5,000, some were kids, some millions, but a lot of people."

The Anointed Son

It didn't take long for Guinn to fire back with a defamation lawsuit.

"Chuck Ruthe essentially stated that Jeff Guinn is a criminal despite the fact that there is absolutely no indication that any criminal investigation is underway or that any criminal charges are even being considered by any authorities," Guinn's attorneys at Bailey Kennedy wrote in September of 2009.

By that time, the FBI had been investigating Jeff Guinn's Aspen Financial for more than four months. A little more than a year later, the Feds would go public with their criminal investigation of Jeff Guinn.

Chuck Ruthe, who invested much of his fortune with Aspen Financial at the urging of Kenny Guinn, would spend the remainder of his life in litigation with the governor's son, a man he had hoped to see behind bars.

32: KILLING THE MESSENGER

When people don't like the story, they blame the messenger. It happens in a variety of professions, but none more than news. "She's biased." "He's been bought." "That one is trying to please her _____ (boss, lover, mother, friend.)" You fill in the blank. I've heard them all.

Sometimes, reporters have an agenda. But sometimes there is no agenda other than to get the story, get it right, and tell it, no matter who it helps or who it hurts. It's the imperative I live by, ingrained in me by the late, great newsman Ned Day, who was Managing Editor at KLAS TV when I was a cub reporter.

Sometimes the story is undeniable. Such was the case when the governor's son turned out to be using Las Vegas police as his own personal enforcers.

Jeff Guinn's legal pleading stated, "Donna Ruthe's good friend, Dana Gentry (who is also a good friend of Steve Quinn) is a producer on the *Face to Face* show hosted by Jon Ralston."

Steve Quinn is hardly my good friend. He is married to my good friend, Vicki Quinn. Let's say Steve and I have had a tepid relationship for decades.

It's true that in the years since I met Donna Ruthe, we have become friends. But when Jeff Guinn's attorneys stated it in legal pleadings back then, I'd met her twice, both times for interviews.

I was annoyed at the lie, especially in a public document, but it wasn't the first time I'd taken heat for a story, though never to this extent. Little did I know it was the first salvo in an attack that would threaten my credibility and my career, and go all the way to the Nevada Supreme Court.

The Anointed Son

Jeff Guinn would soon allege that I was a major player in a conspiracy to destroy him.

33: CASH OUT

One of the more brazen schemes alleged by the Ruthes and other Aspen lenders involved borrower Susan Mardian, who had two corporate entities with loans brokered by Aspen; one for a self-storage facility at Cactus and Bermuda in Las Vegas, appropriately called Aspen Storage, and the other for a nearby condominium complex under construction called the Milano Residences.

On both loans, Mardian, through a variety of entities she controlled, placed third trust deeds on the properties without any evidence of putting money into the project. Those deeds appeared on title a few days or weeks before Aspen would broker another loan, and the Mardian entity claiming an indebtedness on the property would immediately get cashed out.

How much? $7.6 million from the Milano refinances and about $1.5 million from Aspen Storage. In a deposition involving Aspen Financial, Mardian claimed she was taking out equity. It's questionable that she had any equity, given the fact Mardian borrowed the money to buy the land.

Here's how it worked:

In August of 2001, Aspen loaned Mardian $750,000 secured by a piece of land that Mardian's HK Investments owned at Cactus and Bermuda.

A quarter of a million dollars went into a construction reserve account at Nevada Construction Services, but the lion's share of the loan — $400,000 — went directly to Susan Mardian. Less than a year later, Aspen loaned Mardian's HK Investments $350,000, which included interest payments on her two existing loans and cash out to Mardian, who pocketed $227,000.

During the next seven years, Aspen would broker a series of loans totaling $55 million, that included close to $8 million in payments to entities owned by the borrower, Mardian—payments secured by deeds of trust placed on the property weeks, sometimes days, prior to Aspen brokering a new loan.

On July 21, 2006, Mardian's Joshua Tree LLC placed a $1.5 million deed of trust on the Aspen Storage property, in anticipation of an Aspen refinance. Less than two weeks later, on August 2, 2006, Aspen funded a $2 million loan, including $1 million cash out to Mardian, who kindly wrote off the other half a million she'd just attached to the property. Aspen's fee for that loan, which appeared to be created for the purpose of funneling cash to Mardian, was a hefty $61, 250.

The Loan Summary and Investors Authorization on the Milano loans makes no mention of loan proceeds being used to pay off deeds of trust placed by the borrower, but it does describe Susan Mardian's financial condition:

"Guarantors Susan R. Mardian. Susan R. Mardian will also personally guarantee the loan to this company. Ms. Mardian's financial statements reflect a strong net worth. Credit reports were reviewed on Ms. Mardian personally. Which substantiated a responsible credit history. All financials and tax returns are available for review. Tax returns for 2005 will be provided when completed."

Bruce Coin, an expert witness hired by the Ruthes, estimates Aspen earned $1,641,455 in origination fees on just the Milano loans before the pyramid crumbled under the weight of all that debt, a sagging economy and no way to finance yet another loan to pay off the existing debt.

Investor Charles Thompson talked under oath about the Milano loan's costly history of serial refinancing.

Thompson: I think it's more criminal behavior. Because it also includes Ponzi. Because they're using loans from a new loan to pay off another loan, which is what Ponzi is, paying off old debts with new debts. And to learn, even this late in the game, that $7.6 million was given, just written out and paid through cash by the loan broker, who's supposed to trust you, is shocking.

But more than that, there's another side to this, and that is possibly worse, those funds, if not given away -- to my mind, they were given away -- would have completed the project. That project would be sitting there today, no matter what condition it's in, finished.[66]

Retired escrow executive and Aspen lender Jim Zeller took a close look at the Milano loan for his wife, Lois Levy, and expressed outrage at what he found during his December 2010 deposition in the Ruthe case.

Dennis Prince: What did you look at in terms of the Milano loan?
Jim Zeller: Well, first of all, there was a lot of money loaned, and the property never got completed. I went out -- Kenny Gragson and I went out and looked at the property a couple of times, and it was nearly completed. It was not completed. And we started digging, and I think it would have taken approximately $16 million to buy the property and build it.
Q: To complete the project? 16 million more?
A: To buy the property -- to buy the land and build the improvement.
A: Okay.
Q: And it's never been completed. And there's been over $29 million loaned on it. We know that instead of finishing the completion, the Mardians took out over seven-and-a-half-million dollars.
Q: Did you ever ask Lois was she made aware of that?
A: I'm sorry?
Q: Did you ever ask your wife Lois if she was ever made aware of the fact that the Mardians had taken this money out of the project?
A: She is now. But this is all post default.
Q: I understand.
A: She's aware of it.
Q: I know now. But before she made the loan, was she made aware

---

[66]Charles E. Thompson deposition p. 83-84

that the Mardians were taking money out of the project this way?
A: No. Of course not.
Q: Did you see anything else concerning other what you described on the Milano loan?
A: Again, there's unpaid taxes, the property is not completed, and also Aspen has been trying to sell the property for less than $3 million. And that's a long way from the $19 million it is on the first trust deed.[67]

The lawsuit filed by Lois Levy and others against Jeff Guinn and Aspen Financial alleges:

"Upon information and belief, no money was actually loaned by Joshua tree to Milano LLC, nor was anything of value provided by Joshua Tree to Milano, LLC or the Milano property. In this regard, the Joshua Tree Deeds of Trust purport to secure a debt not owed. Nevertheless, on no fewer than three occasions Aspen solicited Lenders to loan money to pay-off the Joshua Tree Deeds of Trust. ... For brokering the $55,140,000 in loans, Aspen received in excess of $1,100,000 in origination fees. In addition to the origination and loan servicing fees, Aspen also received and retained (in apparent violation of the loan agreements) in excess of $130,000 in loan extension fees. This money rightfully belonged to the Lenders."

Susan Mardian's company made its last payment in July of 2008, when the interest reserve ran out on the loan. A forbearance agreement expired February 1, 2009. In October of 2009, Aspen had yet to file a breach against the Milano property.

Mardian wasn't the only borrower to benefit from frequent cash withdrawals courtesy of the Bank of Jeff. Desert Land principal Howard Bulloch was a regular recipient of cash to the borrower.

Jilted Aspen investor Charles Thompson testified in a deposition in the

---

[67] Jim Zeller deposition p.46

Ruthe case about Aspen's two preferred methods for funneling cash to the borrower.

Q: ... my point is, there's similarity in the sense that Aspen allowed the principals of the borrower to take money out of the loan proceeds?
A: They're similar to that extent, except Aspen in one paid them, wrote a check out of escrow, distributed out of escrow the funds.
Q: To whom? One of Bulloch's entities?
A: No, on Milano. In other words, there was a trust deed filed that they paid off to Joshua Tree.
Q: Three trust deeds.
A: Right. In Howard's, I think they just took it right from escrow to him. And I haven't seen the loan borrower statements.
Q: You're saying that in Bulloch's case, they weren't like allegedly paying off a deed of trust. They were just making a payment. But whether they're paying off a deed of trust or just allowing money to be taken out, the loans were similar in the sense that the principals got money out of the loan proceeds that the investors never knew about?
A: That's right.[68]

David Moody is a bank executive in Las Vegas who once worked at Aspen Financial. Dennis Prince asked Moody under oath about the practice of paying the borrower "cash out."

Q: Now, were you aware while you worked at Aspen that when Aspen was either refinancing a loan or putting a second on the property, that they would allow the borrower to take actually money out of the property?
A: I wasn't aware of that.
Q: If you were aware of that, would you have been concerned about it, assuming it did happen?
A: Yes.
Q: Why? Again, because it take equity out?

---

[68] Thompson p. 44

A: It takes equity out.
Q: You agree an investor should be informed if a borrower is going to be taking equity out of the property in connection with a loan?
A: I would assume that would be in the disclosures. [69]

The problem: the disclosures arrived in the mail after the close of escrow. The money was already in the borrower's hands.

That's what Jeff Guinn likely intended, and his business model relied on it.

---

[69] David Moody deposition p. 75

34: A FEDERAL CASE

Jeff Guinn appeared on the FBI's radar on June 8, 2009. records I obtained in 2016 via a Freedom of Information Act request reveal that on that day, the FBI in Las Vegas ran Guinn's driver's license information and received a list of vehicles registered in his name.

Four days later, the FBI received by email a copy of Community Bank's legal motion to protect its collateral. The bank wanted to know the location of the jet plane Jeff Guinn pledged as collateral.

On August 1, 2009, the Attorney General of Nevada, Catherine Cortez Masto, sent the feds copies of documents requested by the FBI.

35: "KAI" UNCOVERED

I love to read court documents. I'm always amazed at reporters who fail to peruse a single motion, then walk into court without knowing any of the players. Court filings are a treasure trove of information. Such was the case when Steve Quinn sued Jim Thomas, Paul Osuch, and Metro.

It was the first week of July 2009. I was two pages into the "Interrogatories" from the federal lawsuit when the name jumped out at me.

Detective Kai Degner, in black and white. Identified in the documents as one of the Metro personnel who ran SCOPE on Steve Quinn.

I called Ray Flynn. His assistant put me through.

"I found him!" I yelled when Flynn picked up. "I found Kai. He ran SCOPE on Steve Quinn. Kai Degner!" I was feeling quite proud of myself.

"Dana," Flynn sounded exasperated. "You're driving me crazy. Kai Degner works for me. He's the detective who did the Internal Affairs investigation of Osuch. That's why he shows up running SCOPE on Steve Quinn."

"Oh," I said, completely deflated. "Sorry to bother you." I couldn't believe how stupid I was.

Then I remembered my conversation with Flynn in December. Metro had two cops named "Kai." One was a patrolman, and the other a detective. Jeff's connection at Metro wasn't a patrolman. He was a detective. Maybe the detective was now in a different department. I believe in coincidences, but with a name like Kai, this was likely more than chance.

I did some digging, made some calls, and got a break courtesy of the same source who gave me Paul Osuch's name. Metro Detective Kai Degner was an investor with Aspen Financial. What's more, it was public record on the Clark County Recorder's website.

36: A WORKING VACATION

I don't get away much, but as luck would have it, in early July 2009, I was about to head to the beach with kids in tow. I packed up the car and prepared for the trip to California. But first, I looked up the phone number for Metro Detective Kai Degner.

His phone went to voicemail.

"Hi," I said. "My name is Dana Gentry. I'm a journalist at Channel 8. Please call me." I left my number and hoped for the best.

It didn't take long before I heard back from Degner. "Hi," I said. "I've been reporting on Jeff Guinn procuring confidential SCOPE information, and I believe you're the mystery detective who was doing Jeff's bidding!"

Silence.

"You need to call the Public Information Officer if you want any infor…" Degner began to respond. I interrupted, fearing he'd hang up.

"Do you know Jeff Guinn? Are you an investor with Aspen?"

"You'll have to call the PIO." *Click.*

I called Flynn from the car. He was on his way out of town, too, and I'm sure I was the last person he wanted to hear from.

"Kai Degner is an investor with Aspen Financial," I said. Then I waited.

"What did you say?" Flynn asked. But I knew he'd heard every word.

"Kai Degner is an investor with Jeff's company. The guy who investigated the dirty cop who was doing Jeff's bidding is an investor in Aspen Financial. And I'll bet you anything he's the same "Kai" that Jeff was calling to have Steve Quinn busted."

"Where did you get that?" Flynn asked.

"None of your business. But it's public record!"

"I'll call you back."

Here's how Kai Degner recalled the incident under oath.

"Uh...she [Gentry] started off by saying that uh... I'm the mystery detective in the Paul Osuch case. Uh... and she... she was trying to... to get me to, uh... tell her whether or not I had a... whether or not I knew Jeff Guinn. Uh...and the specifics from there, my head started spinning at that moment, bring up this case. Uh... so I just... I just kept telling her, any information is gonna have to come from the PIO."

We were about to walk down to the beach when my phone rang. I made a quick check for sunscreen and sunglasses and shooed the kids out of the room, promising to meet them at the pool in a few minutes. Then I took Ray Flynn's call.

"If you ever need a job, you can come work for me," he said, sounding slightly defeated.

"You mean I was right?"

"Yes, Degner admits he was an investor. He's not now. But he was."

"When he was investigating for Jeff? What's next?" I asked, grabbing a piece of hotel stationery to jot down my notes.

"We'll be opening a second internal affairs investigation. It will be two-pronged."

The Anointed Son

"What does that mean?"

"It means we'll look at the new allegations involving Degner and answer all your questions, and we'll go back and review his work on the Osuch case."

Seconds after I hung up, my phone rang again. It was Internal Affairs Detective Daniel Stopke from Metro, wanting to set up a police interview!

"I'm a journalist! I don't get interviewed by cops. Watch the program Friday and you'll hear everything I have to say."

I hung up, corralled my kids at the pool, and took a walk to the beach. Life was good.

37: KENNY TALKS

While I tried to enjoy my vacation, my thoughts were on the story. We had a program scheduled on the topic upon my return. Kenny Guinn had agreed to talk, too. Not on air. And not with me.

My once sterling relationship with Governor Guinn deteriorated rapidly when I began reporting on his son. That's to be expected. Like Jeff, Governor Guinn refused to be interviewed by me.

I was irked that Governor Guinn had agreed to talk with Jon, who didn't know nearly as much as I did about the story, and was in no position to challenge or follow up. (I don't mean to sound conceited. Jon enjoyed extensive knowledge of plenty of topics of which I knew nothing.)

I did my best to prepare Jon with a list of questions:

> Who ran Aspen while Jeff was in rehab?
> Why did Jeff sign an agreement preventing the second trust deed holders from foreclosing on the first in the Flamingo/Town Center loan?
> Why did Jeff have the Quinns followed?
> Who paid for the surveillance?
> How much did the Guinns have invested in Flamingo/TC before it was refinanced? How much after?
> Why won't Jeff talk?

The governor denied taking part in the operations of Aspen Financial while his son was in rehab, and told Jon that Sean Corrigan filled in. Sean Corrigan later testified under oath that the "girls" at Aspen watched the store, adding he didn't think any loans were processed during that time.

The next question involved a loan we had reported on called Flamingo Town Center, a vacant lot on the west edge of town that carried massive debt.

On September 18, 2006, the day before the close of escrow on the final Flamingo Town Center loan, Jeff signed an agreement that essentially eliminated foreclosure as an option for his investors on a $21.85 million second deed of trust. Guinn desperately needed to refinance the existing Flamingo Town Center loan, in which he at one time had close to $9 million of his family's money invested.

Ohio Savings Bank (Amtrust) agreed to fund a new first mortgage. The catch: Guinn had to agree that Aspen's second-mortgage holders would not foreclose if the borrower stopped making payments on the first mortgage.

Predictably, the borrower defaulted on the first mortgage. Aspen Financial attempted to foreclose, despite the agreement. Amtrust sued, and the second-mortgage holders were left without recourse.

Why did Jeff Guinn sign that agreement? That was the question posed to Governor Guinn by Jon.

The governor didn't answer the question directly, but told Jon the Guinn family lost hundreds of thousands of dollars on the second mortgage loan.

Aspen Financial earned approximately $1.5 million brokering the Flamingo Town Center loans.

38: STRANGER THAN FICTION

On Friday, July 10, 2009, we identified Kai Degner on *Face to Face with Jon Ralston* as the Metro cop doing Jeff Guinn's bidding. The intro to my taped story said:

"Here's another one of those stories that sounds like it's out of a bestseller. Governor's son calls police to do his bidding. Police get caught, and the Internal Affairs investigation is conducted by, who else? One of the cops suspected of doing the dirty work for the governor's son."

Jeff Guinn declined to be interviewed—by me or the police.

The Metro Police Internal Affairs report, which I received from Metro after the second investigation, notes that Jeff Guinn's attorney, John Bailey, responded to Metro on July 14, 2009.

"He said Guinn told him he is too busy for an interview and requested OIA submit a list of questions which he will respond to in writing. OIA declined to send questions due to problems extracting accurate statements from Guinn." –Internal Affairs Bureau report

Sometimes truth is indeed stranger than fiction. This had to be one of those occasions.

39: JEFF GUINN

Jeff Guinn seemed like a nice enough guy when I met him through the Quinns. We all went to a party together, a fundraiser for an organization called Street Teens, which helped kids pushed out of their homes get back on their feet.

Jeff Guinn seemed to have a charitable heart.

When thousands of New Orleans residents displaced by Hurricane Katrina headed for Las Vegas in September of 2005, Jon Ralston and I stopped by Catholic Charities to get some interviews for the program.

Guinn was there with a stack of $20 Target gift cards—$10,000 worth, he told me, for the victims who were arriving with the clothes on their backs and not much more. I interviewed him for the story we were doing that night.

Jeff was well-liked by classmates at Western High in Las Vegas, where he excelled as a football player and suffered injuries that would later be blamed for his addiction to painkillers.

He earned a Bachelor of Science in Economics from Arizona State and returned to Las Vegas, where he was a manager trainee at Valley Bank of Nevada.

He became the manager of the consumer loan department and the Loan Administration officer at Nevada Savings and Loan, which would become PriMerit Bank.

In the 90s, after working at Clayton Mortgage, a hard-money lender, Jeff struck out on his own and opened Aspen Financial. If timing is everything, Jeff Guinn's was perfect. He was soon cranking out loan after loan, trying to satisfy the unquenchable desire for growth that gripped Southern Nevada during his father's tenure in office.

The third-to-last time I saw Jeff Guinn, he was sitting with Sean Corrigan in the back of Judge Allen Earl's courtroom. I attempted to approach him during a break to ask a question. He started screaming like a child, "Dana, stay away from me! You're a threat to me! Bailiff, help!"

I was flabbergasted. Jeff Guinn could put on quite a show.

The second-to-last time I saw Jeff Guinn, he performed an encore. He had just testified in his bankruptcy fraud trial. The judge called for a break. As Guinn walked past me on his way out of the courtroom, I rose to ask him a question about his son's allegations of physical and sexual abuse.

"Dana, I told you to stay away from me!" he screamed, loud enough for the judge, who was still on the bench, to hear.

It was an Academy Award-worthy performance.

The last time I saw Jeff Guinn was the Trifecta. It was early September 2017. He had just finished testifying about helping former Aspen borrower Howard Bulloch buy back shares of his defaulted loan for pennies on the dollar.

Following Jeff's testimony, Bulloch's attorney addressed Judge Elizabeth Gonzales.

"Your Honor, we believe someone in the courtroom is taking pictures of Mr. Guinn."

"I'm not taking pictures," I blurted out. "Check my phone."

"I don't think she's taking pictures," added Judge Gonzales, who called for a break.

I walked outside to where Guinn was standing, intending to let him know the book was coming out soon and offering him a last shot at talking.

"Dana, get away from me. I've told you to stay away," he screamed as a bailiff turned the corner. "She always does this!"

The bailiff motioned for me to walk away and admonished Guinn to calm down.

40: A TOWER CAPER

In April of 2005, Kai Degner was a detective in the Las Vegas Metropolitan Police Department's Fraud and Financial Crimes Division. Degner testified in a deposition he met Jeff Guinn that month while on what Degner called "a tower caper." That's police talk for a case involving high-profile figures in the community. Within weeks, Degner fingered the alleged bad guy, an employee suspected of stamp theft at Guinn's Aspen Financial.

Within months, Degner invested $10,000 in an Aspen loan. The relationship with Guinn may have proved briefly profitable for Degner. But in the end, he would pay dearly.

The next time Kai Degner heard from Jeff Guinn was in April of 2006. Guinn was calling about a real estate broker with whom he had a business beef. The broker's name was Kevin Donahoe.

Degner would eventually recall the events under oath:

A: I contacted Mr. Donahoe's attorney to ask if Kevin would be willing to be interviewed. And his attorney, after he got done laughing at me, said, "No, but I'll send you documents over." And he sent me a whole bunch of documents over. A lot of them were the same documents that I got from Jeff Guinn and Kent Barry.
Q: What did you report back to Mr. Guinn after you concluded it was a civil matter?
A: I told him that this appears to be a civil matter, that he should take it up in court.
Q: Were you an investor at Aspen at that point in time still?
A: I can't remember if my last investment had paid off not or yet. I think there was still something going on.
Q: It's your best recollection that as of April 2006, you were still an

investor at Aspen. Is that right?
A: I think so. Yeah, I should have been.
Q: When did your last investment with Aspen pay off, to your recollection?
A: It was in April. I think it was April of '07. [70]

Metro's own Internal Affairs Report quotes several of Degner's supervisors who say a disclosure of his investments with Guinn would have disqualified him from the investigation. Nor did Degner notify his superiors of his involvement in Guinn's business when he was assigned cases involving Guinn in 2006 and 2007.

The Internal Affairs detectives asked Degner if he "thought his investment could have posed a conflict with him initiating and conducting a criminal investigation on a company with which he had an investment."

"No, because I... I bank with Bank of America, and I did investigations for Bank of America too. Uh.. they'd have tellers stealing money, their... the documents tell the story in Financial Crimes, just like with Osuch, the off lines told the story," Detective Degner told OIA.

But when Internal Affairs appointed Degner to the Osuch case, he notified his supervisor, Sgt. Kelly McMahill, of possible conflicts. Here's how McMahill recalled the conversation to the Internal Affairs Bureau:

"In this situation, what I recall... and again, I'm going back to October of 2008, um... I recall Kai getting the case, reviewing it, which is standard, coming to me and saying, 'Just so you know, I'm aware of the parties involved in this case.' And I said, 'What do you mean by that?' He said, 'I've had some prior dealings with Guinn. Uh... and this... this will become confusing for transcription because it's Guinn and Quinn. In this case he said to me, 'I've had some dealings with Jeffrey Guinn,

---

[70] Kai Degner deposition p. 72

um... from my time in Fraud.'"

"I remember very specifically saying, 'What do you mean by involvement?'
And he [Detective Degner] said, 'Well my name is gonna show up in these off line searches.' And I said, 'Okay, why?' He said, 'Well I took a report from Guinn, uh.. he was the victim if I'm remembering correctly, and as part of that I ran somebody [Quinn] involved.' And at the time I didn't even know who he ran. There was so many people we were doing off line searches on. So my question to him that day was 'Did you run this person [Quinn], or is your name part of this off line search for work related reasons, or personal reasons? He said no, it was all work related."

McMahill says she decided to let Degner keep the case. Once exposed, Degner confessed to McMahill just how far Guinn's tentacles reached. The Internal Affairs report quotes McMahill on learning from Degner about a phone call Degner received from Guinn.

"So again, I'm taking notes and he says to me, 'there's another thing that I have to add, um... and that...' and I said, 'what?' Cause I'm thinking, it's bad enough. He said, 'um... while the Osuch case was ongoing, I got a phone call from Jeff Guinn asking me about the case, the status of the case, and he said, but I... I assure you I did not give him any information.' When I heard this I looked up again at Kai and I said, 'Why did you not immediately come into my office after that phone call and tell me?' And his response was, 'I don't know.' Uh... at that point I... I said, 'we have to end this conversation,' because I realized we were moving past any Contact Report being written, and it was a prelim investigation I was doing with him."

How did Jeff Guinn know Degner was investigating the Osuch case? It's one of the questions that has puzzled me most.

Did Osuch tell Thomas, who in turn told Guinn? And if so, what chutzpah on Jeff Guinn's part to pick up the phone and call him!

Degner would later change his story about Guinn calling him during the

The Anointed Son

Osuch case, claiming instead that he was talking about earlier investigations. However, his statement to Sgt. McMahill leaves little room for doubt that Degner was talking about the Osuch case.

Degner told Internal Affairs that Jeff Guinn, while his father was governor, badgered Degner about filing criminal charges against the younger Guinn's foes. But Degner's interview with Internal Affairs reveals he was all too willing to indulge Jeff Guinn, going so far as to obtain a secret grand jury subpoena for bank records and even conferring with the District Attorney's office.

Detective Degner told OIA that Guinn was calling him repeatedly encouraging him to file a criminal complaint with the Clark County District Attorney's office against Donahoe in reference to the second event. ... Detective Degner said "I conferred with the District Attorney's Office, they agreed with me that this whole mess was civil, so it was closed to civil. Uh... Guinn was pissed off and he kept calling me for months trying to get me to ... to submit this as... as a Criminal Complaint. And I... I believe I... I even spoke with uh... Sergeant Napier about it and we ended up sending him a letter saying, you know, this... this is nothing. It's civil."

Detective Degner also told OIA Guinn's motivation for calling him repeatedly.

"He... he [Guinn] was trying to get uh, ... a Criminal Complaint on Donahoe because he [Guinn] was being sued to try and discredit Donahoe. And by using our investigative, uh... claiming that he, that Donahoe had stolen money from him would make Donahoe look like a ... a liar, cheat, and a thief."

In deposition, Degner testified about Guinn's reaction to Degner's characterization of the alleged crime as a civil matter.

A: He wasn't happy.
Q: How did you know he wasn't happy? What was he telling you?
A: He said that this was criminal and it should be going to the D.A.'s

Office.
Q: What did you tell him in response to his statement that it's criminal and it should be going to the D.A.'s Office?
A: I told him with what I had in front of me at the moment, that it was civil. I was still waiting on some type of statement from Kent Barry. But with what I had at the moment, it was a civil matter.
Q: What statement were you waiting for from Kent Barry?
A: I was waiting for a written statement from him detailing all the transactions.
Q: Did Mr. Barry ever provide that statement to you ever?
A: I don't remember if he did or not. If he did, it didn't come to anything. I don't remember. ...
Q: After April 25, 2006, say up until April of 2007, let's use that one-year time period, how frequently would Mr. Guinn call you about Kevin Donahoe and wanting you to pursue the matter as a crime?
A: There was sometimes he would call me a couple times a week. Sometimes I wouldn't hear from him for several weeks. ... He would rant and rave. I would tell him with what I have, it's still civil. And we would hang up.
Q: Did he tell you why he wanted you to pursue the criminal complaint so aggressively?
A: Because he thought Kevin Donahoe was stealing from him.[71]

Degner testified under oath that he became annoyed by Guinn's calls.

Q: Did you think he was trying to unduly pressure you to doing something that you otherwise would not want to do?
A: He's no different than many other victims. You know. People lose money, they, I don't consider it unduly. It got to be annoying.
Q: I thought you said in your statement he started to piss you off?
A: Yeah.
Q: Why was he pissing you off?
A: Because he kept calling. ... I just remember the phone calls. I don't

---

[71] Kai Degner P. 74 – 75

remember the actual conversations. I remember getting lots of phone calls from him telling me that he wants this thing done as a criminal complaint. And it wasn't -- the facts weren't there. I'm not going to submit a criminal complaint on someone that doesn't deserve a criminal complaint.[72]

But Degner's testimony reveals that not only did he go to the District Attorney to appease Guinn, but he also sought a grand jury subpoena to obtain Kevin Donahoe's bank records.

Here's what he told Steve Quinn's attorney Dennis Prince under oath:

Q: Did Mr. Guinn, between April of 2006 and 18 April of 2007, ever contact you indicating he thought Mr. Quinn was engaging in criminal activity?

A: Not Mr. Quinn being engaged. He thought that Kevin Donahoe was somehow in cahoots with Precision. And to that end, when I got the grand jury subpoena back from the bank account, I looked for any connections and there was none.

Q: What grand jury subpoena?

A: I did a grand jury subpoena on Commercial Specialists bank account.

Q: In connection with which investigation?

A: With the investigation of Donahoe.

Q: So you got, was Commercial Specialists, were they notified of the subpoena on their bank account?

A: No.

Q: So a grand jury, you can use a grand jury subpoena to secretly obtain documents without the customer or the deposit holder knowing it?

A: Uh-huh.

Q: Is that a yes?

A: Yes.

Q: Really? I didn't know that. Would that grand jury subpoena have been issued sometime in April of 2006, before you closed it out as a civil matter?

A: I don't remember when it was issued.

---

[72] Kai Degner deposition p. 78

Q: After you closed it out in the civil matter, as a civil matter, there would really be no reason for you to have a grand jury subpoena issued, would there? (Ah, good point!)

A: I don't remember at what point we did the grand jury subpoena.

Q: I know that. Let's think about what the likelihood of it was.

If you close something out as a civil matter, does that suggest to you, Officer Degner, that the likelihood is you had the grand jury subpoena issued before you closed it out as a civil matter and you had access to those bank records?

MR. LENHARD: Form. Calls for speculation.

BY MR. PRINCE:

Q: Go ahead and answer.

A: I don't remember when we did the grand jury subpoena. I closed it out early because it appeared to be a civil matter. But we continued having communication with him. And until I got a statement from Kent Barry, there was still the possibility of a criminal complaint. So like I said, I don't know when I did the grand jury subpoena. I usually try and get them done fairly early on though.

Q: Would it have been your custom and practice to have the grand jury subpoena issued, go get the bank records and review those before you close something out as a civil matter?

A: Most of the time, yes.

Q: Any reason to believe you didn't do that here?

A: Like I said, I'm not going to sit here and tell you I did or I didn't. Because I don't remember when I did it.

Q: At any point between April of 2006 and April of 2006, did anybody, Mr. Guinn tell you, ask you to run Steve Quinn? ...

A: No.

Q: You ran Mr. Quinn through Scope, appears on October 2, 2006. Correct?

A: Yes.

Q: Why?

A: That would have been in connection with my investigation of Donahoe.

Q: But what information did you get about Steve Quinn between April

The Anointed Son

25, 2006 and October 2, 2006 which would lead you to run Mr. Quinn through Scope?

A: That would have been when I had the bank records and Jeff Guinn intimated there was some connection between the builder and Kevin Donahoe.

Q: When would he have done that?

A: After, sometime after I took the initial crime report.

Q: So why wouldn't you run Mr. Quinn before April 25, 2006, when you closed the matter as a civil matter?

A: Because I didn't have a need to.

Q: How did you develop a subsequent need to?

A: I don't remember.

Q: What information did you have about Steve Quinn after April 25, 2006?

A: What do you mean?

Q: What information did you have about Steve Quinn after April 25, 2006, if any, as it related to Kevin Donahoe?

A: There was nothing there. There was no connection.

Q: Then why run him?

A: I ran him as a part of the investigation to see who all the players are.

Q?: According to the notes, you don't even reference him in at all, in your report. Then why run him?

A: Because I was told that he was somehow connected with Kevin Donahoe.

Q: How come you wouldn't have known that in April, that Mr. Quinn is somehow connected with Mr. Donahoe in connection with a property management issue?

A: Because sometimes it takes time to develop information.

Q: I thought you told me there was no new information that came to you after April 25, 2006?

MR. LENHARD: I think that misstates his testimony. Object to the form.

THE WITNESS: Guinn was constantly calling me telling me more, different things, trying to get me to make a criminal complaint.

Q: What did he tell you about Steve Quinn?

A: I don't remember.

Q: Then why run him through Scope?...
THE WITNESS: Because I still had an investigation that I was dealing with.
BY MR. PRINCE:
Q: What active investigation was going on in August of 2006, when you had already closed it out as a civil matter, as of April 25, 2006?
A: It may be closed in the system. It doesn't mean it's gone away. I'm still getting phone calls on it.
Q: Earlier, you said he wasn't giving you any information, he was pissing you off, he was annoying you, he wasn't giving you new information. Kent Barry hadn't come forward. Then why run Mr. Quinn if that's how you felt?
MR. LENHARD: He's answered that now about four times.
MR. PRINCE: Okay, go ahead and answer.
MR. LENHARD: Answer the fifth time, if you would. Or ask to have your answer read back. Whatever you want.
MR. PRINCE: Well, no. Kirk, please, just object to the form. I got your objection.
MR. LENHARD: You can't keep asking the guy the same question over and over again trying to get a sound bite. I'm not going to sit here and put up with it.
A: Because with each of those phone calls, I was still having to deal with that case and whatever information he relayed to me.
Q: When did you contact Mr. Quinn about that investigation?
A: I didn't.
Q: Why?
A: Because there was nothing there to link him to anything.
Q: How do you know?
A: Because I had the paperwork in front of me.
Q: When did you get the paperwork in front of you?
A: Between the two, Jeff Guinn and Donahoe's attorney and then the grand jury subpoena, there was nothing there linking Commercial Specialists to Precision Construction or anyone else.
Q: Well, you would have likely had that information, according to your earlier testimony, as of April 25, 2006. Did you learn anything new after

April 25, 2006 about Steve Quinn or Precision Construction?
MR. LENHARD: *Same objection. Asked and answered.*
BY MR. PRINCE:
Q: *Go ahead and answer.*
A: *Not that I remember.*[73]

I'd like to think Detective Degner would have conducted just as thorough and lengthy an investigation for any citizen. But something makes me think that kind of service is only available to alleged victims of a "tower caper."

41: JUDGE GONZALEZ

Governor Kenny Guinn appointed Judge Elizabeth Gonzalez to the Clark County District Court in 2004.

In the summer of 2009, Gonzalez found herself presiding over one of three cases in which Aspen investors were suing the governor's son. She was also the judge in a suit Aspen filed against Community Bank of Nevada, alleging the bank breached its agreement to finance tenant improvements for a shopping center at Horizon Ridge and Green Valley Parkway in Southern Nevada.

All the Guinn/Aspen loans from Community Bank contained a cross-collateralization provision. If one loan went bad, they'd all be considered in default. That meant the former governor, who joined his

---

[73] Kai Degner p.82-90

son as a guarantor on another loan with Community Bank, had a stake in that lawsuit. Yet the bank never objected to the Guinn-appointed Gonzalez hearing the matter.

Not so for Aspen investor Lois Levy, her husband Jim Zeller, and retired attorney Charles Thompson and other plaintiffs who alleged in a July 2009 court filing that Gonzalez failed to disclose her relationship to Guinn and wanted her to step down.

Judicial ethics require judges to put certain relationships on the record before rendering any decisions so that litigants are fully informed and able to assess their options.

In an affidavit, Gonzalez claims she didn't disclose because the plaintiff's attorney should have remembered opposing her in 1988 when Gonzalez represented Southwest Gas, which was run at the time by Kenny Guinn. And she says it's a matter of public record that Guinn appointed her to the bench in 2004.

It was a controversial move for the judge to retain the case. Judicial canons suggest judges should avoid any appearance of impropriety. But Gonzalez held her ground. It sounded like perfect fodder for the TV show I produced, *Face to Face with Jon Ralston*.

The tease wrote itself: *Plaintiffs in a lawsuit against the son of former Governor Kenny Guinn want Judge Elizabeth Gonzalez off the case for allegedly failing to disclose her relationships to Guinn and his son, Jeff. Did the judge, a former member of the Nevada Ethics Commission, satisfy rules governing judicial disclosures? Plus, how often does a judge's failure to disclose potential conflicts interfere in the quest for justice?*

I put in a call to the judge, just on the remote chance that she'd address the controversy. No go.

Did Gonzalez disclose her relationship to the governor in the Community Bank case? I requested a video copy of the hearing from the court. Not all, but some Clark County court rooms are equipped with cameras, which record all the proceedings. It's the greatest thing the county has ever done for reporters.

The video record in the Community Bank case, in which the governor had a stake, revealed Gonzalez made no mention of her relationship to Kenny Guinn.

But at one point during the hearing, the judge called the attorneys to the bench for a sidebar.

Sidebars, of course, are meant to be private conversations among the judge and lawyers. To my delight and amazement, the county's recording of the proceedings included the audio of the sidebar.

The recording captured the judge telling the attorneys, off the record, that "the Ralston Show" had called about cases involving Guinn. She stopped short of telling the attorneys not to talk.

I asked but never heard back from the judge on why she notified the attorneys of my call.

On July 30, 2009, we aired the program about Judge Gonzalez and showed viewers her sidebar warning to the attorneys about the Ralston show.

Shortly thereafter, the court instituted rules regarding the use of side bar material captured on the court's official recording.

Also on July 30, District Judge Allan Earl denied Guinn's motion to dismiss the Ruthe suit.

Jeff Guinn had seen better days.

Guinn's attorney went to court in August to fight the disqualification and keep Gonzalez on the case. Guinn's attorneys alleged in their motion the Levy et al plaintiffs were using the media to stir the controversy.

"The plaintiff's recent use of the Jon Ralston show as a medium to publicize their motion sheds further light on its impropriety and lack of merit," the Aspen attorneys wrote.

"If a party were allowed to selectively disqualify a judge through what amounts to media-bullying, the very integrity and independence upon which the judiciary depends will be undermined."

Eventually, Judge Art Ritchie allowed Gonzalez to stay on the case.

It was the first time Guinn's attorneys, John Bailey and Dennis Kennedy, would play what would become an all-too-familiar refrain. It was about to get ugly. Bailey and Kennedy, presumably acting at the insistence of their client based on what I had seen from Jeff Guinn, were about to engage in media-bullying of their own, threatening the "very integrity and independence" upon which the First Amendment depends.

42: GREED AND REVENGE

In September of 2009, Jeff Guinn filed a counterclaim alleging defamation against Donna and Chuck Ruthe. Guinn said my "good friend" Donna Ruthe enlisted my help to get the story out.

Forget the fact that I met Donna Ruthe the first time I interviewed her in November 2008. No one had to enlist my help to get this story out. It's simply a great story. My imperative as a journalist, drilled into me from the time I was a young reporter by the late Ned Day and my mentor and former boss, Bob Stoldal was this: get the story, get it right, and tell it, no matter who it helps or who it hurts.

Jeff Guinn alleged in his counterclaim that Donna Ruthe, with help from me and the Quinns, filed a lawsuit out of greed and revenge, not because Aspen Financial Services owed the Ruthes and their family members some $7 million.

"The story Plaintiffs/Counterdefendants have concocted regarding complicated real estate transactions is nothing more than a misguided attempt at misdirection. Specifically, it is an attempt by Donna Ruthe, the mastermind of this lawsuit, to use the cover of an undisputed international, national, state-wide and local economic meltdown and this lawsuit to mask ulterior motives.

This lawsuit, filed by plaintiffs, is about greed and revenge. For years, Donna Ruthe has been attempting to unconscionably bleed Chuck Ruthe—her husband—out of his individual property and deprive his children of an inheritance he had planned for them. When Jeff Guinn refused to help Donna Ruthe with her money grab and later fired her for her incompetence and unprofessionalism, she sought revenge. As she has done with others in the past, Donna Ruthe is and has been attempting to destroy Jeff Guinn by conducting a public smear campaign against him and his company (Aspen) behind the shield of a baseless and improper lawsuit." ...

And this:
"Donna Ruthe then asked Jeff Guinn to assist her in her efforts to get control of Chuck Ruthe's money. Jeff Guinn refused to help Donna Ruthe. ... Donna Ruthe wanted, and continues to want, revenge."

In an effort to dispel the Ruthes' contention that they were misled by Aspen and Guinn, Bailey argued that the Ruthes knew the risks and detailed the company's compliance with a seminal law, part of what he called "Aspen's business processes."

"Aspen is required by law to make certain disclosures to potential investors and Aspen complies with all applicable laws regarding such disclosures.

As part of Aspen's business processes, **before** *a potential investor can participate in any loan, Aspen requires that investors read, understand, and acknowledge receipt of a Mortgage Investment Disclosure Form.*

....

Prior to participating in any loan *with Aspen, investors must attest that they have read, received and understood the Mortgage Investment Disclosure Form." (Emphasis added)*

Four years later Jeff Guinn would contend under oath that he had a license to break that very law, impeaching his own attorney's pleadings in the process.

43: The Harmon Fallout

Harley Harmon was a hard money lender and a member of a prominent Nevada family, convicted of 34 counts of mail fraud that involved bilking investors of millions of dollars. In 1998, an interim committee led by a promising young Democratic Assemblyman named David Goldwater produced a measure intended to protect consumers from another Harmonesque failure.

Assemblyman Goldwater, who would eventually become a hard money lender himself, told the Las Vegas Sun back in 1998 that investor backed loans were critical to the Southern Nevada economy, but noted the abuses alleged in the Harmon case.

"We really, really want to protect the investor in this process," Goldwater said. *"They are unsuspecting. They are attracted by high yields, and they need to be protected. I want to work to make this a great industry for the state of Nevada." –Las Vegas Sun, 1998*

Among the members of that interim committee charged with shoring up the law was Jeff Guinn, whose father Kenny was running for governor of Nevada.

During a hearing on the critical disclosure documents, Guinn suggested that mortgage brokers, not title companies, be responsible for ensuring their timely execution.

Fourteen years later, the governor's son would audaciously testify in deposition under questioning by Dennis Prince that while his dad was in office, state officials gave Aspen Financial permission to ignore that law, a seminal provision he helped write. It was a provision that, if complied with, would have alerted Aspen investors to the troubled deals Jeff Guinn was peddling.

Dennis Prince: Now, before accepting the money, did Nevada law require Aspen as a hard money lender to have the investors sign any documents or disclosures?
Jeff Guinn: There was a lot of change on that I think in '06, or

something like that.
Q: What do you mean '06?
A: I think that's when they put that law into effect.
Q: What law?
A: The statute. What you just said.
Q: Okay. So in 2006, Aspen was required to give the written disclosures to the investor and have them sign it before—
A: Well, Aspen wasn't required. But was that a statute within the new laws when they changed them, yes.
Q: Well, it's Aspen's obligation to comply with those laws. Right?
A: Yes. But that law was supposed to be changed because it was not feasible with all the hard money lenders. And it was something that was causing a tremendous problem with the State, because you have people that were out of town and signing documents maybe afterwards. And they knew that wasn't feasible, and they were supposed to have it changed in the LCB after the Legislature. And I think at the time they were in between commissioners and it didn't get done.
Q: So you're saying that a law went into effect that later was supposed to be changed?
A: Yes.
Q: Did that relieve you of the obligation to comply with the law's requirement?
A: The State was not enforcing it, and with any mortgage company because it created a terrible problem that you couldn't do business.
Q: So your point is – well, tell my why you couldn't do business?
A: Let's say you have a rollover of $50,000, and you want to go on this loan. And you say, well, I'm out of town. I can't get the documents to you. Just send them to me and I'll get them back to you. Or someone comes in and says 'Look, I got to take the documents home and have my husband sign or my spouse sign. Here's a check. Get the position funded. And I'll bring it back. And they forget about it for three or four days. The loan funds, and then you have a problem. And so the regulators knew that that was impossible to do business for the mortgage brokers. And every mortgage broker got together, the regulators would understand that that wasn't an issue.

Q: So you're saying—who are these regulators?
A: You need to talk to them.
Q: I'm asking you who the regulators were. You're the one who's —
A: The Mortgage Lending Division.
Q: Who are you working with at the Mortgage Lending Division that said you didn't have to comply with the law's requirements?
A: They were the ones saying that they weren't going to enforce that because it created a problem, and they knew it should have been changed and it didn't get changed. I'm just telling you what they told me years ago.
Q: Who are these regulators that told you that?
A: I think it was one of the commissioners. I can't remember his name.
Q: What do you think his name was?
A: I don't know if it was Scott Bice or the guy after Scott Bice. I'm not sure.[74]

Guinn's contention that he was somehow excused from obeying the provisions of a seminal law seem, oh, I don't know—absurd! Nonetheless, I sought out these obsequious regulators.

I queried not only Scott Bice and his successor, Joe Waltuch, but also their predecessor, L. Scott Walshaw, who ran the state's Financial Institutions Division, the agency that spawned the Mortgage Lending Division. I also checked with the current administration. Not one person knew of the "terrible problem that you couldn't do business," to which Guinn testified under oath.

"To suggest that regulators allowed licensees to ignore the law is inconceivable," said Joe Waltuch, MLD Commissioner from September of 2007 to February 2011, when he was fired by Governor Brian Sandoval.

Scott Bice was the MLD Commissioner from 2003 to 2007. He now

---

[74] P. 186 - 187 Jeff Guinn deposition May 2013

works for HUD in Atlanta.

"It was the law—the law is the law in that it must be complied with, so no "outs" to anyone," Bice said, adding that he was also unaware of any problems with compliance.

Compliance with the state law on disclosure forms *would have* provided Aspen investors with information they required to make sound investments. But contrary to Guinn's attorney's assertions, their client claimed he had state sanctioning to break the law.

I asked then-Attorney General Catherine Cortez Masto, the official who held the authority to charge Guinn criminally back in 2013, about Guinn's blatant disregard of the law, but never heard back.

Cortez Masto is currently a U.S. Senator.

44: PONZI SCHEME?

In December of 2005, Aspen Financial provided Las Vegas developer Mark Oiness with two loans totaling $40.9 million, almost 100 percent financing, to acquire land at the west edge of the Las Vegas valley. The parcel at the intersection of Flamingo and Town Center was planned for senior living units as well as commercial development.

Public records reveal the Guinn family and Aspen Financial held $8.9 million or 34.25 % of the $26 million first mortgage. *Investment Guys*, an LLC controlled by Jeff Guinn and his father, Governor Kenny Guinn, held 4.67% ($1,214,200.00) at the close of escrow.

The Guinn interests sold almost all their 40 percent share—all but one percent—within ninety days.

Why did Guinn and family get out?

Maybe, as Jeff Guinn would later testify under questioning by the attorney for the bank he turned to for a bailout, it's because he had concerns about the value of the collateral before he brokered that loan in December 2005.

Amtrust Attorney Elise Lavelle: So you had a concern in December, January, February that the market was such that the value of this property was not going to be where you thought it was going to be; is that right? Or where you'd hoped it was going to be?
Jeff Guinn: We knew it wasn't going to be where it was 18 months, two years before when we did the loan first.[75]

---

[75] Ohio Savings Bank (Amtrust) v. Aspen, August 2008

Guinn appears to have never shared his concern regarding values with his investors.

To get the massive loans off its books, Aspen turned to Ohio Savings Bank (Amtrust), which refinanced most of the Aspen-brokered first and second mortgages into a new, first position loan.

That allowed Aspen to broker a new second position loan of $21.8 million in September 2006.

Under the gun to get the loan refinanced and earn the lucrative origination fee, Guinn agreed to Amtrust's demands for the new loan — an "intercreditor agreement" that prevented the second mortgage holders from foreclosing on the first in the event of default. Aspen Financial points out its investors signed subordination addendum, a document giving Aspen Financial:

"...the power to execute and deliver any subordination agreement duly requested in writing by Borrower and meeting the requirements set forth above, together with such other documents as may be reasonably requested by Borrower including but not limited to any agreement with such construction lender to Borrower."

An examination of the loan file reveals many of the subordination addendum and disclosure documents were signed after the close of escrow, in violation of the law.

Aspen Vice-President Elaine Elliot, asked under oath in 2016 whether she notified investor/lenders of the existence of an "intercreditor agreement" that prevented lenders from exercising their recourse to foreclose, replied "It's not one of the documents I've been instructed to pass on through the closing package."

Lenders on the Aspen-brokered second mortgage would eventually get wiped out, including the Guinn family, which lost a couple hundred thousand dollars of the close to $22 million venture.

The Anointed Son

While the lenders were out of luck, Aspen earned $1.7 million in origination and servicing fees on the Flamingo Town Center loans.

We aired the story in July of 2009, with a clip of Jeff Guinn testifying in the Amtrust lawsuit about negotiating a forbearance agreement with Amtrust in 2008.

Jeff Guinn: You know, there may have been some discussions on the fact that we had—Mark had wanted us to do a new loan on the project, on Flamingo/TC, and we were concerned about the values just in the overall real estate market... So we've had discussions before that Mark was having some issues or maybe some value issues, because just the general market as a whole was down. And both of us wanted to make sure where we're at on the value, that it was okay. ...

Guinn, who clearly admits he knew the "market as a whole was down" as early as 2006, would claim in later legal proceedings to have been oblivious to the pending decline.

Q: Had you in fact entered into intercreditor agreements requiring standstill provisions that would require a second deed of trust holder not to foreclose ahead of the first?
A: I don't believe so. ...
Q: Okay. Now, let's assume for just a minute that AmTrust said to you, you know, you've got to sign this intercreditor agreement with the subordination and the standstill, or we won't—we won't loan the money as a first. Let's assume that was said. Was that what was said? Do you know?
A: At the beginning—
Q: Sure.
A: -- the middle or—I mean—
Q: At any time.
A: Well, if you already have a loan outstanding, you're kind of at their mercy.
Q: Why?
A: It's take it or leave it.

Q: Why is it take it or leave it? If you've already got a loan, Aspen's already made a loan; is that right?
A: Correct.
Q: And you don't disburse funds without a deed of trust being in place; correct?
A: If Amtrust doesn't make a loan, the second probably won't be made, either.
Q: All right. But then the second may be a first; correct? Can't you get enough money together to make a first instead of a second, since you're in that business?
Mr. Forstadt: Objection, Your Honor.
The Court: Overruled.

Elisse Lavelle, attorney for AmTrust, was spot-on.

Guinn couldn't put enough money together to make that size of a loan, unless he put Guinn family money on the line. And with the economy souring, he wasn't about to keep that kind of money in a loan much beyond the time it took to close escrow. Finding enough new money to sell those assignments was getting tougher.

That was the day AmTrust attorney Elisse Lavelle characterized Jeff Guinn's business model as a Ponzi scheme.

45: Regulator Roulette

Cheryl Rogers Barnett filed a complaint with the Nevada Mortgage Lending Division in the summer of 2009, specifically about the Flamingo Town Center loan, in which Guinn, the day before the loan closed, relinquished the rights of his own investors on a second trust deed to foreclose on the first. It's an agreement that robs investors of their recourse in the event of default.

The state of Nevada's reply to Barnett's complaint in September of 2009 noted that Guinn was within his rights to sign that "intercreditor agreement," and Michael D. Haley, Compliance Audit Investigator, pointed out the provisions of the loan were clearly detailed in an Investor Summary Sheet. Mr. Haley's letter states:

To explain the risks of loaning money secured by deeds of trust and to inform investors of other rights provided under Nevada law, Aspen was required to provide all investors with a Mortgage Investment Disclosure Form, which among other things required that Aspen disclose either its involvement, or a relatives' involvement, with any entity for which Aspen brokered the loan.

Mr. Haley noted he did not review the lender documents, along with disclosure forms detailing the lenders' rights. Had he done so, he may have noticed the documents, including those critical disclosure forms, were mailed to investors for signatures on September 19, the day the loan closed.

That's a violation of NRS 645b.195, the state law that requires those documents be signed before the broker accepts any money.

September 19, 2006

ROGERS-BARNETT FAMILY TRUST
CHERYL & LARRY BARNETT, TTEES
PO BOX 577
WASHINGTON, UT 84780

Re: Investor Documents

Dear Investor(s):

Enclosed you will find your investor documents and information folder. Please sign all documents as indicated by the signature tabs. A return envelope is enclosed for your convenience. Copies will be sent to you for your files.

If you have any questions, please contact our office at 341-8499 or 1-888-341-8499.

Milli Ventling
Investment Operations Department

The Anointed Son

Haley also noted that the Power of Attorney Mrs. Barnett signed gave Aspen the right to subordinate her interests. Had Haley looked at the actual document, he may have noticed Barnett's Power of Attorney is dated September 29, 2006—ten days after the close of escrow.

We told Barnett's story on *Ralston Reports* in February of 2010.

Dana Gentry

46: I'll be Watching you

Journalists enjoy striking a nerve. I learned in November of 2009, a year after the first story on Jeff Guinn, that I must have struck gold.

The call came from Jon Ralston.

"Dana." It was a tone of voice Ralston seldom used, reserved for the thankfully rare occasions when I really screwed up.

"Someone's been hired to follow you," he said.

"What?"

I thought he said someone had been hired to follow me.

"You heard me," he went on.

Apparently, Susan Mardian, the borrower on one of Jeff Guinn's loans, the Milano project, had approached a former Metro cop and inquired about hiring someone to watch me. The source told Ralston that Mardian was hoping to have me pulled over after leaving a bar, arrested for DUI, and disgraced. Bad call, since I don't drink. I've never even had a glass of wine or a beer.

As luck would have it, the former cop Mardian approached had told someone who knew me and Jon to let us know.

"What do I do?"

"Obviously, you are on to something," Jon answered. "Keep digging."

I was overcome with a sense of satisfaction. The Mardians seemed to be borrowing a page from Jeff Guinn's book. Or more likely, they appeared to be in cahoots with Guinn.

I called the person who tipped off Jon and thanked him. He wanted me to watch two or three cars behind me and in an adjacent lane to see if anyone was following me. I agreed to try, which I did. Briefly.

It's not easy to drive while watching two or three cars back in another lane without an eventual collision with the car ahead. At least, for me. My stint as a PI was short-lived, brought to a halt before it cost anyone a bumper.

Let Mardian waste money paying someone to follow me. I'll admit it was slightly unnerving, but the knowledge that they were motivated to shut me down made it worthwhile. Plus, my life was dull. Let them learn it firsthand.

I warned my kids not to do anything stupid. And I did what Jon told me. I kept digging.

47: Neglect of Duty

Former Metro Sgt. Paul Osuch accessed confidential Department of Motor Vehicle records 227 times for Jeff Guinn's private investigator, Jim Thomas.

"It's the most I'm aware of. I mean, by far. You know, I mean, we discipline people for running somebody once, and this was a couple hundred times," Assistant Sheriff Ray Flynn testified under oath during Steve Quinn's lawsuit against Metro Police in January 2010.

In 2008, Flynn, who supervised then-Internal Affairs Detective Kai Degner, told me, "We may never know who Kai is," apparently failing to make the connection between his own detective and the mysterious "Kai," identified by Donna Ruthe on *Face to Face* as Guinn's man at Metro.

As it turned out, Detective Kai Degner, who was conducting the Internal Affairs probe into how Jeff Guinn obtained hundreds of confidential reports from Metro, was not only doing Guinn's bidding, he had also invested with Aspen Financial.

Flynn told Steve Quinn's attorney Dennis Prince that Metro sustained a complaint against Kai Degner for Neglect of Duty for failing to report his financial relationship with Guinn.

"… I would have hoped that an investigator would have had the forethought to let us know that they had a financial arrangement with an individual that was concerning one of their investigations."

Flynn also testified that the police found no deficiencies in Degner's original IAB probe of Paul Osuch, the cop who was assisting Guinn's private eye.

That's remarkable, given Kai Degner's statement to his supervisor, Sgt. Kelly McMahill, that Guinn called Degner during the Osuch investigation.

How, I wonder, did Guinn know Degner had the case? No one at Metro went out of their way to ask.

Flynn also testified that the investigation turned up no evidence of surveillance conducted on Guinn's behalf by Vice or Narcotics.

Attorney Dennis Prince asked Flynn if anyone asked Kai Degner about the alleged surveillance.

Flynn: I'm sure.
Prince: What did he say?
Flynn: I don't know what he said.

48: EYES ON MILANO

The FBI file on Jeff Guinn and Aspen Financial is replete with redactions, but the agency failed miserably to protect the identities of some of its own agents, among them Special Agent Steve Konrad, whose name and initials appear throughout the document.

On March 23, 2010, Special Agent Konrad met with an unidentified Assistant U.S. Attorney and provided him with an update on some of the allegations made against Aspen, including:

- Use of inflated appraisals
- Self-dealing by Jeff to protect his financial interests and others at the expense of investors
- Refinance transactions used to generate fees and pay interest reserve
- Improper use of interest reserve

Konrad and the AUSA went on to discuss two loans. The first was Flamingo TC, in which investors alleged that without their knowledge, Guinn made a side deal with the bank holding the first mortgage that the holders of the second mortgage he brokered would not foreclose. Investors claimed Guinn's side deal robbed them of recourse in the event of default.

The FBI file entry notes:

"SA _____ and AUSA _____ agreed that in the event that this agreement was not disclosed, it probably was not material to the investors in their investment decision making process."

While that may be true, the feds appear to have ignored the illegality inherent in the lack of disclosure.

The two decided the best course of action was to pursue a different money trail—the one leading to Milano.

49: FAR AND WIDE

Jeff Guinn's attorney, John Bailey, frequently referred to Aspen Financial critics as a small band of disgruntled investors, confined to Charles Thompson, the Ruthes, and a few rogues under their influence. The truth, which is revealed in FBI documents I obtained, is that Aspen's detractors were many and from a variety of locales.

On February 22, 2010, investors in Thayne, Wyoming, who believed they'd been defrauded by Aspen, sent a letter to the FBI asking that the feds put a hold on Aspen's dealings pending appointment of a receiver.

The Wyoming investors would eventually involve their U.S. Senator, Republican Mike Enzi.

On March 4, 2010, an investor from Sun Valley, Wyoming wrote to the FBI, inquiring as to why none of Aspen's borrowers were being held to their personal guarantees.

On April 13, 2010, the Portland complaint line of the FBI received a call from a woman claiming to have lost $3.8 million in Aspen investments.

On May 19, 2010, the persistent investors from Thayne, Wyoming wrote that they were following up on previous correspondence concerning what they called "Aspen Financial criminal actions."

"We have had correspondence with Wyoming's 2 Senators, Wyoming's Congresswoman, Wyoming Attorney General, the director of the Security and Exchange Commission, U.S. District Judges Alan B. Johnson, Will F. Downes, Clarence Brimmer, U.S. Attorney General, The Federal Trade Commission and the Nevada Attorney General. We have received replies from all our correspondence except the Nevada Attorney General and Nevada's FBI office and we are concerned that our correspondence was received."

The Anointed Son

In 2010, Catherine Cortez Masto was Nevada's attorney general. Today, she is a U.S. Senator. Cortez Masto has declined to be interviewed regarding Aspen Financial.

The Wyoming investors went on to say:

"We think Aspen Financial is being operated as their personal piggy bank, instead of a financial institution. (Madoff?) If something isn't done soon to protect investor lender's assets, there will be no assets left."

On September 15, 2010, a man who identified himself as a retired pilot told the FBI he and four or five friends had lost $3 million with Aspen. The man said he had consulted a postal inspector who suggested he contact the FBI. The man asked to bring a group of friends to talk with agents.

On September 20, 2010, the FBI received an email from a woman in Utah who alleged Aspen was operating a Ponzi Scheme.

On September 22, 2010, Helen Peabody of Visalia, California visited the FBI office in Las Vegas. Peabody is an elderly woman who told the FBI she enjoyed some success brokering her own hard money loans. When she learned of Aspen Financial, and that it was owned by the son of Nevada Governor Kenny Guinn, Peabody decided to let Guinn do the brokering for her. Today, she and her husband, a retired law enforcement officer, are still fighting to recoup their life savings.

In June of 2010, the FBI in Las Vegas busted a syndicate of Southern Nevada real estate agents in an alleged mortgage scam. For some reason, the Las Vegas Sun newspaper account of that incident is included in the FBI's file on Aspen Financial. Perhaps the FBI suspected a similar scam in the works at Aspen, on a commercial scale.

A nationwide sweep that targeted mortgage fraud across the country has resulted in 123 people in Southern Nevada being charged, convicted or sentenced in connection with the probe.

The announcement was made Thursday at the Lloyd D. George federal courthouse in downtown Las Vegas. The investigation was dubbed Operation Stolen Dreams.

Authorities said the defendants allegedly engaged in hundreds of "straw buyer" transactions involving hundreds of Las Vegas area properties with a total loss of more than $246 million.

Officials said 73 of the 123 suspects in the case worked in the local real estate industry, including 30 loan officers, 24 real estate agents, six loan processors, five settlement agents, four mortgage brokers, two appraisers and one builder. Charges against 72 of the 123 suspects were filed this week, U.S. Attorney's Office spokeswoman Natalie Collins said.

The Southern Nevada Mortgage Fraud Task Force conducted 25 criminal investigations during the probe.

"Those 25 identified criminal investigations are just the beginning and comprise just a portion of the Mortgage Fraud Task Force's active case and current work load," U.S. Attorney for Nevada Daniel G. Bogden said.

Other investigations are expected in the coming months.

"The Southern Nevada Mortgage Fraud Task Force still has hundreds of cases to investigate," said Kevin Favreau, special agent in charge of the Las Vegas FBI office.

Nationwide, the probe has resulted in officials identifying 1,215 defendants resulting in about 500 arrests with alleged losses surpassing $2.3 billion, officials said.

Southern Nevada has been especially hard hit with mortgage fraud.

"Very few of the offices within the FBI have seen as much fraud in the real estate industry as we've seen here in Southern Nevada," Favreau said.

The Greater Las Vegas Association of Realtors released a statement this afternoon praising officials for investigating fraud in the industry and saying its 12,500 members are barred from participating in the kind of schemes alleged by prosecutors.

"We support and cooperate with such efforts by local, state and federal regulators and law enforcement agencies to aggressively investigate and prosecute anyone in the real estate industry suspected of fraud," association President Rick Shelton said in the statement. "The fraudulent activities alleged by the Southern Nevada Fraud Task Force are harmful to homeowners, law-abiding members of the real estate industry and the public at large. GLVAR members receive the highest level of professional training and must abide by a strict code of ethics that prohibits such behavior."

While this nationwide effort to stop mortgage fraud began March 1, the local task force was formed in 2008 after the FBI noticed an increase in the number of complaints during the summer of 2007, Favreau said.

When home prices began to fall in Southern Nevada, it became more difficult for criminals to carry out their scams, officials said.

FBI Supervisory Special Agent Scott Hunter said many of the homes involved in the scams eventually went into foreclosure.

"They used these houses kind of like ATMs," Hunter said of the alleged scammers. "They took as much money out of them as they could, and when they were done taking the money out they left it and basically left Southern Nevada in a wreckage."

The alleged fraud artificially inflated home values in neighborhoods where the scams took place, leading to innocent homebuyers overpaying and having a higher chance of foreclosure when the economic hardships hit, Hunter said.

Agencies that participated in the Nevada probe include the FBI, the U.S. Housing and Urban Development Office of the Inspector General, the U.S. Postal Inspection Service, the Secret Service, the IRS Criminal Investigation unit, the Social Security Administration's Office of the Inspector General and Metro Police. — Las Vegas Sun, June 17, 2010

The FBI file included a few other surprises, including biography-like material on Nevada Governor Brian Sandoval and some news stories on real estate deals involving George Chanos, the former Nevada attorney general appointed by Guinn to fill a vacancy left when Sandoval briefly took a position on the federal bench. Chanos says he has no clue why the FBI was investigating a connection between him and Aspen Financial, and asserts there was none. He also says he holds Kenny Guinn in the highest esteem.

Sandoval's office did not respond to my requests for comment.

50: Desert Land

On July 13, 2010, the Securities and Exchange Commission informed the FBI that it was closing its file on Aspen Financial.

"... the SEC will not be pursuing an investigation into Aspen at this time. Per _____ the sale of partial interests in deeds of trusts by Aspen to _____ does not fit the fraud statutes in which the SEC has jurisdiction as it appears that appropriate discourses (probably meant disclosures) were made in the loan documentation."

The SEC's investigation clearly did not include a review of the disclosure forms required to be signed by Aspen lenders before they invest any money. Those forms were routinely signed days, even weeks, after loans closed escrow, a clear violation of Nevada law.

The SEC may have had no interest in Aspen Financial, but the FBI was expanding its investigation to include another loan.

On August 26, 2010, the FBI received a call from a man identified in FBI records only as Aspen Financial's attorney. Counsel for Aspen informed the FBI that Aspen had shredded documents for the three earliest Desert Land loans, but would provide a letter of explanation to the Grand Jury.

It was the first indication that the Grand Jury had broadened its investigation beyond the Milano loan.

A few weeks later, on September 9, 2010, FBI records reveal an unidentified person met a federal agent at the Starbucks at Decatur and Sahara in Las Vegas and turned over a video copy of *In Business Las Vegas,* which included my recent story on the Desert Land loan, secured by Las Vegas Boulevard property across from the Mandalay Bay. The multimillion-dollar loans resulted in no improvements to the property, but did put millions in "cash out" in the pocket of the borrower, Howard Bulloch.

51: Tragedy Strikes

On July 22, 2010, Kenny Guinn climbed a ladder, his wife Dema says, to blow pine needles off the roof of their Las Vegas home.

The coroner would report that it was unclear whether Guinn suffered a medical event that caused him to fall from the roof or whether the fall killed him. Dema Guinn, who discovered her husband's body, told RJ columnist Jane Ann Morrison she begged the former governor not to do the chore, but he insisted.

"I heard the ladder scrape over the concrete and I went outside. He was on the ground, his hand on his chest. He was dead." She rushed to hold her husband of 54 years in her arms, but there was no time for words, she said Saturday, in her first interview.

She remains shattered, but made one request.

"Tell the love story Kenny had with the state," Dema Guinn said between tears and sobs.

"He cared so much about the people of Nevada; he cared about the people who couldn't make their house payments, people who couldn't put food on the table, seniors, children. Every morning and night he worried about the state."

Despite his son's troubles, Kenny Guinn remains a highly regarded and respected man in the state he helmed well beyond his death. His legacy, the Guinn Millennium Scholarship, which offers $10,000 to any Nevada student with a qualifying grade point average, has doubled the number of students who remain in the state for higher education.

The last time I saw Kenny Guinn was in March of 2010, when he appeared on Ralston Reports. As I walked him out of the studio, the former governor, who always agreed to come on the program when asked, but who was none too happy with my reporting on his son's company, looked at me and said, "That will be the last time." And it was.

52: THE FEDS SQUEAL

The FBI isn't in the habit of announcing what it's up to. In the case of Aspen Financial, it did.

According to FBI records I obtained, on November 4, 2010, an Assistant U.S. Attorney met with the Ruthes' attorney, Dennis Prince. After the meeting, the AUSA told a special agent to obtain questionnaires from Milano investors to determine if "material misrepresentations/omissions were indeed made by Aspen employees in the solicitation process."

On November 10, 2010, the FBI sent letters to an unknown number of Aspen's thousands of investors, requesting information on:

"investments and association with Aspen Financial Services. Please provide as much detailed information as possible, and forward the completed questionnaire to the Las Vegas Field Office of the FBI, by December 10, 2010. ….

The Victim Notification System (VNS) is designed to provide you with direct information regarding the case as it proceeds through the criminal justice system."

Contact information followed, and after that, a two-page questionnaire.

The FBI questionnaire made its way to me by mid-November. Was it real? I put in a call to the FBI contact listed on the document, who confirmed its authenticity.

I read it again and more carefully. Number 5 caught my eye.

"Did you invest in a loan commonly known as the "Milano" loan?"

The other questions seemed lame.

What the document lacked was the seminal question: *When were your disclosure documents signed—before or after the close of escrow?*

Still, it was quite remarkable.

53: When Donna Slapped Dema

Donna Ruthe says she was pushed. And then it happened.

The slap heard throughout the state.

I listened to my voicemail as I left Channel 3 on November 9, 2010 after Ralston Reports, around 7 p.m.

It was Donna Ruthe. "Dana, I just slapped Dema Guinn." *Click.*

I called her back immediately.

"You what?"

"She shoved me and I slapped her. It was like a reflex."

"Where did you see her?"

"At Southern Highlands, after Maddy Graves' funeral."

"You slapped the first lady at a funeral? Jesus, Donna."

I didn't need to tell her how bad it looked. She knew. No need to rub salt. Dema Guinn would take care of that.

The former First Lady obtained a protective order, proclaimed her fear of Ruthe, and managed to separate Ruthe and her wheelchair-bound, Parkinson's disease-afflicted husband Chuck from their gun permits, at least temporarily.

I tried to get details or a comment through Jeff's attorney. Nothing.

Las Vegas Review-Journal columnist Jane Ann Morrison wrote the story.

Jane Ann called me about it, which I thought was strange. I told her the truth—Donna left me a message saying she slapped the First Lady but said she was provoked.

Jeff Guinn's attorneys would allege in court documents that I attempted to kill Jane Ann's column. It was yet another wholly-manufactured allegation. It simply never happened.

PHOTOS

Governor Kenny Guinn talks with journalist Jon Ralston and Steve Quinn in route to Elko, Nevada aboard a timeshare jet paid for by Aspen Financial. Photo courtesy Vicki Quinn

Governor Guinn, Vicki, and Steve Quinn. Photo courtesy Vicki Quinn.

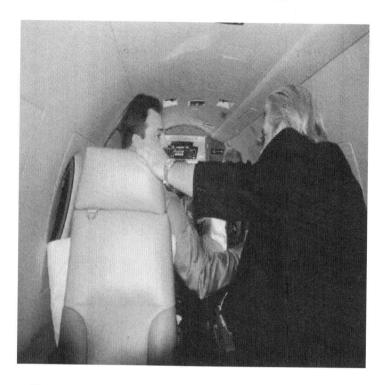

Jeff Guinn talks with Steve Quinn aboard a flight on Aspen's timeshare plane. Photo courtesy Vicki Quinn.

The Aspen Opening package, which contained important disclosures required by Nevada law to be signed before investors turned over their money to Aspen Financial, should have been sent to prospective lenders before the loans closed escrow. Instead, Aspen routinely sent the Opening package and Closing package together after the close of escrow. Aspen employees fraudulently notarized the documents, often making them appear to have been signed before the close of escrow.

The Anointed Son

Milano Residences, LLC
Related Parties
Loan# 50-00047-7

Total Loan = $ 19,240,000

Investor#	Investor Name	Principal	Investor %	Relationship
7	Clorie Gill	23,552.18	0.1224126%	Family Friend
48	Carl Krepper	368,596.88	1.9157842%	Family Friend
411	John & Shirley Blair	22,957.92	0.1193239%	Employee Family
606	Noel Rees	35,000.00	0.1819127%	Family Friend
675	Michael Ramsey	50,000.00	0.2598753%	Employee Friend
723	Holly Rees Sgro	17,000.00	0.0883576%	Family Friend
861	Linda Rieke	30,629.44	0.1591967%	Family Friend
907	Gary & Linda Ricke	11,888.31	0.0617896%	Family Friend
1034	Clorie Gill Trust	11,310.00	0.0587838%	Family Friend
1093	Nicholas Steffora	54,864.41	0.2851581%	Employee Family
1132	Tania Steffora Trust	50,000.00	0.2598753%	Employee
1137	Aspen Mortgage, LLC	5,486.09	0.0285140%	Related Entity
1330	Gary Rieke Trust	150,000.00	0.7796258%	Family Friend
1590	Janice Seiler	35,000.00	0.1819127%	Family Friend
1906	Howard Bulloch Trust	325,000.00	1.6891892%	Family Friend
2073	Linda Gill	25,000.00	0.1299376%	Family Friend
2102	Anthony & Linda Pusateri	30,000.00	0.1559252%	Family Friend
2107	William & Shannon McBeath	500,000.00	2.5987526%	Employee Friend
2393	Gary Marrone	162,000.00	0.8419958%	Employee Friend
2763	Michael Ramsey	50,000.00	0.2598753%	Employee Friend
2837	Adam Corrigan Trust	240,000.00	1.2474012%	Employee Family
2993	Robert & Holly Silvestri	50,000.00	0.2598753%	Family Friend
3005	William & Lily Markham	28,000.00	0.1455301%	Family Friend
3124	John Redmond	300,000.00	1.5592516%	Family Friend
3682	Richard Doptis	90,000.00	0.4677755%	Employee Family
		2,666,285.23	13.86%	

Guinn prepared this document to illustrate to the FBI that his friends and Aspen employee's family members lost money in the Milano loan. Note the absence of Guinn family investment and the relatively small amount held by Aspen friends and family compared to the total loan amount.

Monica Guinn at the beach. Photo courtesy Vicki Quinn.

Dema Guinn (seated in hat) and cosmetic surgeon Benjamin Rodriguez.

The Anointed Son

Aspen Financial investors Donna and Chuck Ruthe.

Chuck Ruthe interviewed by Jon Ralston on Face to Face in 2009.

Former First Ladies Dema Guinn and Dawn Gibbons on Christmas Day 2016. (Facebook)

The Anointed Son

First Lady Dema Guinn and Governor Kenny Guinn hand out candy for Halloween.

Developer Garry Goett, Donna Ruthe, Dema Guinn, Daralynn Goett, Chuck Ruthe, and Governor Guinn at the Governor's Mansion.

Las Vegas home built by defaulted Aspen borrower Howard Bulloch.

Jon Ralston and Dana Gentry on the *Face to Face* set at KLAS TV.

… The Anointed Son

U.S. Department of Justice

United States Attorney
District of Nevada

333 Las Vegas Blvd. South   Telephone (702)388-6336
Suite 5000   Fax (702)388-5087
Las Vegas, Nevada 89101

May 7, 2012

Las Vegas, NV 89101

Dear Ms.

This letter is to advise you that you are a target of a Federal Grand Jury investigation of criminal violations of federal laws including Title 18, United States Code §§ 1341, 1343, 1344, 1349, 1956 and 1957. If you are interested in resolving this matter short of an Indictment, please have your attorney contact the undersigned at

If no contact is made with our office prior to May 17, 2012, the matter will proceed in the ordinary course of prosecution.

Sincerely,

DANIEL G. BOGDEN
United States Attorney

Assistant United States Attorney

The FBI target letter.

Aspen Financial borrower Susan Mardian, like Jeff Guinn, had problems with prescription painkillers, according to this testimonial.

54: ONE SIZE FITS ALL

On January 26, 2011, an attorney from Aaron Maurice's office whose identity is masked in the FBI file conversed with the FBI via email.

The message raises three interesting points.

1. Some investors believed Aspen didn't pursue personal guarantees for fear of exposing its own loans (and the flaws therein) to scrutiny.
2. Jeff Guinn, the writer surmised, wanted to release Susan Mardian from her personal guarantees in an effort to maintain their alliance.
3. An attorney for the Mardians told the writer of the email: "Everyone knows why developers went to Aspen. All the loans were the same."

55: KAI DEGNER DEPOSED

Jeff Guinn often skipped proceedings in his litigation with Donna Ruthe. He rarely appeared for court motions and depositions of other witnesses.

Guinn, however, was on hand when Kai Degner took the hot seat.

Degner is the former detective who conducted the Internal Affairs investigation into how Jeff Guinn managed to obtain hundreds of confidential background checks from Metro through his private detective, Jim Thomas.

Degner failed to disclose to his superiors at Metro that he had invested with Guinn, nor did he mention how Jeff Guinn urged him to file erroneous criminal charges against Guinn's foes in lawsuits. Those revelations (reported by me) resulted in an internal investigation of Degner's internal investigation.

Degner, deposed by the Ruthes' attorney, Dennis Prince, on February 2, 2011, testified that he was coming face to face with Guinn that day for the first time in years.

Prince began by asking the defrocked detective what happened when he was transferred out of Internal Affairs.

Degner: I was working out of Quality Assurance. ...
Prince: What was your position in Quality Assurance? Did you have a title?
A: To sit at a wall and look at it.
Q: Other than sitting at a wall and looking at it, did you have a position? Do they have a title that goes along with it?

A: They just put me there while they investigated me. ... [76]
A: Captain Minor told me that I was going to be transferred no matter what because they can't have anyone with even a hint of impropriety in our past. So whether I'm cleared of all allegations and everything comes back clean, no matter what, because you decide to go on TV and make this public, and that would make it a, there would be a hint of impropriety against me, they decided they weren't even going to try and keep me.
Q: When you say I went on TV, are you talking about me, that I went on TV?
A: Yes, you.
Q: When did I go on TV and discuss your issues?
A: When you went on John Ralston's show.
Q: What did I say about you?
A: You accused me of being a dirty cop. What exactly you said, I don't remember. I haven't seen that thing in years.
Q: I thought the producer, Dana Gentry, is the one who found out about the issue. Isn't that what happened? (Thanks, Mr. Prince)
A?: Like I said, I don't remember all the particulars of the show. But you were on there and you made the allegations.
Q: Okay. So it was because of me going on the Ralston show there was a hint of impropriety, and therefore you couldn't stay in the Professional Standards Bureau?
A: Yes.
Q: Why couldn't you stay in Quality Assurance?
A: Because that's part of Professional Standards.
Q: You don't investigate complaints like you did in Internal Affairs in Quality Assurance. Right?
A: Correct.
Q: But still, just because there was an allegation of impropriety, it was on that basis alone, whether it's true or not true, that you needed to be transferred out?
A: Correct.

---

[76] Degner p. 6

Q: Did you consider that a form of discipline?
A: No.
Q: Did you consider it a demotion?
A: No.
Q: Did it change your pay grade in any way?
A: It changed my pay.
Q: How did it change your pay?
A: I lost eight percent.
Q: From going from Professional Standards -- were you a detective then?
A Yes.
Q: So you lost eight percent as a detective going to become a patrol officer in the Downtown Area Command?
A: Yes.[77]

Dennis Prince asked Kai Degner about his attempt to question Metro Sgt. Paul Osuch back in November of 2008. Osuch is the cop who was leaking police background reports on unwitting Las Vegans to Jeff Guinn's private eye.

Q: So what did he say to you after you read him his admonishment?
A: He said he was fucked by a friend.
Q: Did he say anything else?
A: Not that I remember.[78]

Degner also detailed his conversation with his supervisor, Sgt. Kelly McMahill, when she became aware of Degner's relationship with Guinn.
McMahill is also the wife of now-Assistant Sheriff Kevin McMahill.

A: She asked if I had any investments with Jeff Guinn's company. And I said yes. And then she asked did Jeff Guinn ever ask me to do anything

---

[77] Degner p. 13 -14

[78] Degner p. 106

for him. And I said yes.

Q: What did you tell Sergeant McMahill that Jeff Guinn asked you to do?

A: She didn't ask me after that. She said, "We're going to end the interview here. I'm not going to ask you anymore questions because you're going to need a representative."

Q: So did she admonish you?

A She didn't admonish me. She just said this is probably going to turn to SOC and go to your office.

Q: What's an SOC?

A: Statement of Complaint.

Q: Did someone initiate a Statement of Complaint against you?

A: Sergeant McMahill did.

Q: What was the basis for that Statement of Complaint?

A: Pretty much everything you people said on the Ralston show.

Q: Which is what?

A: That I was giving information to Steve Quinn. [I think he meant Jeff Guinn - ed.] That I had an unlawful investment. I was disseminating information to private investigators and anyone who would call me. That I had done a shoddy investigation into Paul Osuch. Just about anything you could imagine.

Q: Then what happened after that? Then the Statement of Complaint got filed and they completed their investigation. What's the next thing that happened?

A: The next thing that happened was a couple hours later I was called in to Lieutenant Miyama's office, told I was being transferred. That I was not allowed back into Internal Affairs. That I should start cleaning my office out right then. That if these allegations are true, I should start looking for a new job. If they're not true, at the very minimum I should start looking for a new home within the department. But they figured I would start looking for a new job.

Q: After the Statement of Complaint was filed against you, did you have any contact with Jeff Guinn?

A: Not until the day he walked in here.[79]

---

[79]Degner p. 114-117

Chapter 58

56: TO TAKE THE FIFTH?

With multiple civil lawsuits pending and a criminal investigation hanging over his head, the last thing Jeff Guinn wanted to do was "take the Fifth."

On January 11, 2011, Aspen filed a legal motion noting "it is apparent that an active and ongoing FBI investigation is under way."

Aspen was seeking a protective order to put depositions in the civil suits on hold pending the culmination of the federal criminal probe. The filing also revealed a grand jury was on Aspen's case.

"On or about Aug. 4, Aspen was served with a grand jury subpoena requesting documents regarding the Milano loan."

"In or around November, defendants became aware that the FBI was contacting Aspen investors by letter regarding the Milano loan."

The District Court hearing on Guinn's motion to put his depositions on hold pending the outcome of the FBI probe took place at 9 a.m. on Valentine's Day of 2011.

John Bailey's then-associate Brandon Kemble argued in pleadings that Aspen investor Charles Thompson's "blind obsession" with Guinn was behind the litigation, the FBI probe, and "a public smear campaign."

In addition, Mr. Thompson and the Ruthe Parties—in coordination with some of the Plaintiffs in this matter—have attempted to brow-beat every state and federal agency who will listen to Mr. Thompson's weak theories into opening an investigation of Defendants, all despite their longstanding record of exemplary compliance with state laws regulating Aspen's business practices.

Through their consistent pressure and misinformation, Mr. Thompson and the plaintiffs were finally able to convince one agency—he FBI—to open an investigation into the Milano loan that is the subject matter of this litigation.

Kemble went on to argue about the negative perception caused by invoking the Fifth Amendment, adding this footnote:

Due to Mr. Thompson's coordination with the media in this matter and in particular through the development of a media mouthpiece who is a local television program host, it is likely that any assertion of the right against self-incrimination by Defendants or Aspen employees would be presented to the public, at Plaintiff's prompting, in the most unfavorable light possible.

Bailey et al were taking the sport of Killing the Messenger to a new level.

57: THE HAZARDS OF THE RACKET

It's called "litigation privilege," and it amounts to a license to lie — technically, it's a privilege to not be liable for factually untrue information — in the one place where truth is supposed to prevail: the courtroom.

In late summer of 2011, I was served with a subpoena to produce documents proving a negative — that I was not for sale, that I had not accepted free remodeling work, and that I had not been threatened by the Quinns to hire their son, Paul, or have my "secrets" exposed by Vicki.

The only nugget of truth was that I'd had remodeling work done. I'd called Steve Quinn to see if he would fix a leak in my master bath shower and rip out and replace some other stuff in the process. It was November of 2009, and the market was slow. Steve said no, but added that he was laying off some workers and to talk with them. Steve's longtime (and by then, former) employee Todd Markwart gave me an estimate, the best of three I'd obtained, and we agreed on a price. Steve Quinn was not involved. But clearly, whoever was following me had seen Todd's work van outside my house and run the plate, which had come back to Steve's company, Precision Construction.

My first instinct was to show the proof, any proof I could find, that I wasn't for sale. How does one prove a negative?

I had receipts for the remodel and could show I'd taken a loan from my 401k to pay for it.

Jon Ralston wanted me to sue for defamation. I explained to him that litigation privilege is absolute and allows attorneys to couch their lies by prefacing with "Upon information and belief..."

The same statements, made anywhere else, would have been defamatory. But in court or legal documents, those otherwise libelous utterances are protected. There was nothing I could do.

Ralston argued I was wrong. I maintained that I was right. And I was.

As outlandish and potentially damaging as the "stories for money" allegation was, it was the lie about Paul Quinn that really pissed me off.

I'm not the easiest person to work with, and I have a hard time keeping producers. Paul Quinn graduated from film school in 2010 at a time that I was desperate to find a producer for *Ralston Reports* (the latest iteration of *Face to Face with Jon Ralston*) and *Vegas Inc.*, the business program I anchored and produced.

Not only were Jeff Guinn and John Bailey impugning my character, but they were dragging down a young professional who not only earned his position, but performed well, too.

The allegation about Vicki threatening me was purely fabricated, without a shred of truth.

We'd had a falling out, but it was over something else, not Paul's job.

The fact that Guinn and Bailey had taken whatever sliver of information they heard and attempted to transform it into blackmail involving Paul's job was truly beyond the pale.

Even though not a single allegation made by Guinn was true, it was at times incredibly painful to read. I established a pattern that remained predictable for years. Each time Jeff Guinn's attorneys filed a brief or motion with increasingly egregious allegations against me, I would read it in astonishment and cry for a day or two. I'd then get mildly angry for about the same length of time and eventually become reconciled that it was all part of the territory. "The hazards of the racket," as my father used to say.

My dad, a professional athlete, gambler, and Las Vegas casino

The Anointed Son

executive, had been the target of more than a few false allegations in his time, providing me with a roadmap since childhood on how to cope. I only wished he were still around to give me a refresher.

I once read that fathers shape their daughters' self-esteem at a very early age. My father made me feel like I could do anything. I'm not a religious person. I neither believe nor disbelieve in God or a hereafter, as I've seen no evidence either way. But with false allegations in public documents and my reputation and career on the line, though he'd been gone for two decades, I felt my father's presence and relied on the strength it gave me.

58: THE GREAT AND POWERFUL EARL

I'm not a fan of going to court, and have a history of untimely paid traffic tickets to prove it. But there was more at stake on that December day in 2011 than a speeding infraction.

I put on a black suit to match my dark mood and met my attorney, Don Campbell, at his downtown Las Vegas office, not far from the courthouse. He told me what to expect at the hearing. As much as I abhorred being forced to appear, I wasn't afraid of losing. I didn't see how I could.

The worst that could happen was that we'd lose the motion and I'd be ordered to prove I wasn't for sale and have the opportunity to present my evidence.

I almost hoped to lose in court so I'd be forced to reveal the proof. At the same time, I was tremendously grateful for Don Campbell's time and effort. He knew the issue at hand was important. I trusted he was right.

Judge Allan Earl was a respected jurist and, from all I can tell, a good man. I spent hours in his courtroom watching him play referee between the Guinn and Ruthe attorneys.

On this day, I was the topic, which is a horrible position for a journalist. It was brutal.

John Bailey painted me as a mercenary, a hired gun out to break every ethical imperative I held dear.

I was having trouble keeping my mouth shut. I wanted to raise my hand like a school girl and hope the judge would call on me so I could rat out the lying John Bailey.

Little did I know, the judge was about to call on me.

But first, Don Campbell eloquently made my case, without my help.

The Anointed Son

"You don't drag news gatherers into a courtroom based upon this very, very scant and slender showing which is punctuated by nothing more than what would otherwise be defamatory material about this very, very well-respected reporter and producer."

Then the judge stated his concern for my reputation as a reason to turn down Guinn's request! Could he have come up with a worse reason? It was surreal. He even called me up to the podium, where I stood next to Don Campbell.

In the end, Judge Earl quashed the subpoena. But it hardly mattered once he delivered the Coup de Grace — an admonition not to report on the case lest I be called back before the court for an evidentiary hearing. It would "look better," said the judge.

"Now I'm going to tell you because you're a news person what my wish is. It is not my order, I would never, ever order such a thing. It is my wish — it's not a threat; you understand that?"

"It is my gentle wish that this case be tried in front of a jury and decided and not tried in television programs. Now, you may do what you wish, but that is my wish. We're going to have to pick a jury out of this community that knows absolutely nothing about this case and to sit for days and days and days and ferret out all the testimony and give each party the benefit of the doubt until they have decided which way to rule. That is more important to me than anything, even your career."

"You can go out today and report this any way you want; that's your right under the Constitution, and it's your right in your profession. But the less you are involved in this, the better it is for this decision."

Did I hear that right? Couldn't be.

"I'm sorry. I didn't hear you," I said, disbelievingly.

"I said the less you are involved in this in the future, the better it is for this decision concerning the subpoena."

I was uncharacteristically silent. There was no way I would agree to drop the story.

While the words from the judge were chilling, winning the legal motion by those standards would have been to lose the war. It simply never occurred to me to stop reporting.

Don Campbell was pleased with the victory, but taken aback by the judge's admonition. Campbell told me to keep doing what I had been doing.

To say I was grateful to Campbell, and to Jon for recruiting him, is beyond understatement. I fully realized that without the support of Campbell, Jon, and my longtime boss Bob Stoldal, to whom I owe my career, Guinn and Co. would have succeeded in ending it.

The victory was short-lived. Just days later, right before Christmas, Guinn appealed to the Nevada Supreme Court. It was the third appeal Guinn's attorneys turned out that year, including an effort to postpone depositions in the many civil cases against Guinn until the FBI concluded its investigation.

With a criminal probe in the works, Guinn didn't want to be forced to testify and say something that could be incriminating in a federal case, nor did he want to "take the Fifth" in the civil litigation and let jurors draw their own inferences.

The second appeal that year was in the Aspen v. Ruthe case.

The third, Aspen v. District Court (Gentry), bore my name even though I was not a party to the case.

Like most people, I've always believed litigants are sworn to tell the truth in legal pleadings. False. Legal pleadings and courtrooms are the two places it's safe for lawyers to lie.

And they do.

If nothing else, thanks to Jeff Guinn, I read legal pleadings in a completely different way now.

The Anointed Son

Here are some of the straight out lies Guinn's attorneys alleged in their appeal:

231. Upon information and belief, Dana Gentry assisted Donna Ruthe as a personal favor to her friends Steve Quinn and Vicki Quinn.

232. Upon information and belief, Dana Gentry also helped Donna Ruthe prepare her lawsuit in order to manufacture a news story through which Donna Ruthe could embarrass, harass and defame Jeff Guinn.

233. Dana Gentry improperly, and with bias, shared communications she had with Jeff Guinn and/or his attorneys and Aspen's counsel with Donna Ruthe in order to further Donna Ruthe's plan to get revenge on Jeff Guinn and Aspen through a public smear campaign.

263. Vicki Quinn knew that her friend Dana Gentry would compromise her status as an alleged independent reporter in order to help Donna Ruthe and Chuck Ruthe use their litigation to obtain access to the media in order to attempt to destroy Jeff Guinn and Aspen.

356. Vicki Quinn and Steve Quinn have continued to provide personal favors to and improperly leverage with their close personal friendship with Dana Gentry so that Dana Gentry will continue to assist the Plaintiffs, Steve Quinn, Vicki Quinn and Charles Thompson in their plan to abuse the legal system for their ulterior purpose.

357. Upon information and belief, Dana Gentry continues to work with Plaintiffs, Steve Quinn, Vicki Quinn and Charles Thompson to push Plaintiffs' lawsuit in the media in an attempt to smear Jeff Guinn and Aspen.

358. Dana Gentry intentionally omits facts, improperly vets information, and/or fails to retract or correct the statements she has made on her television and media broadcasts regarding unquestionably false allegations in Plaintiffs' lawsuit in an effort to assist Plaintiffs in their abuse of legal process.

359. Dana Gentry has recently admitted that she is a close, personal friend of Donna Ruthe to other members of the media.

360. Dana Gentry recently called other members of the media in an attempt to get them to spike stories or revise the reporting they had done regarding an assault and battery committed by Donna Ruthe and Chuck Ruthe against Jeff Guinn's mother.[80]

How I wished Guinn had opted for an evidentiary hearing rather than a Supreme Court appeal. A closed hearing before Judge Earl, as the judge offered, would have been a lot quicker, and would have revealed the truth. Instead, the case would drag on for almost two more years.

---

[80] District Court Case No. 09-A587791 v. EIGHTH JUDICIAL DISTRICT COURT OF THE STATE OF NEVADA, IN AND FOR THE COUNTY OF CLARK, PETITION FOR EXTRAORDINARY WRIT RELIEF

59: "WE DON'T NEGOTIATE WITH TERRORISTS."

It was late December of 2011 when Jon Ralston sat down with our boss, Las Vegas Sun publisher and editor Brian Greenspun. Jon explained that Don Campbell provided his services pro bono for the District Court hearing to quash the subpoena issued to me. But just filing the brief for a Supreme Court appeal was expensive—$25,000!

Jon called me after the meeting. He said he'd briefed Brian on the hearing, the appeal, and the issues at stake. After listening for ten to fifteen minutes, Greenspun stated that he didn't get the issue nor did he see a problem was with me answering questions. Greenspun told Jon that John Bailey, Guinn's attorney, also represented him. He even suggested I agree to answer five questions posed by Bailey. If the answer to all of them was "no," I'd be done. The appeal would be dropped.

Huh? I could just imagine the questions, designed to elicit an incriminating "no!"

Jon told Greenspun he'd talk with me and get back to him.

The talk with me didn't go well. I told Jon I'd find a way to pay Campbell for the appeal, but I was not going to play ball with Bailey. Jon wholeheartedly agreed.

A few days later, Jon called Greenspun with a response.

"We don't negotiate with terrorists."

60: NOTARY FRAUD

My stories on Aspen were drawing attention from disgruntled investors in Nevada and, thanks to social media, throughout the country.

It was a seemingly minor infraction. But, as was the case with robo-signing in the mortgage meltdown, notary fraud was a key to the allegations against Guinn and Aspen Financial.

If you've ever been required to have a document notarized, you know the role of notary—the person with the stamp—exists for one reason: to ensure you, the signer, are who you claim to be.

Anyone needing a document notarized must appear before the notary. No exceptions.

An Aspen investor in New York saw my story on notarized documents being signed after the close of escrow, not before, as required by Nevada law.

The investor, Kimberly Casey, says she never set foot in Aspen Financial, where her loan documents were repeatedly, fraudulently notarized. She even supplied receipts proving she was in New York, not Las Vegas, on the days her documents were notarized.

Another woman, Mary Ann Arminio, who lived in the Northeast United States, said she'd never been to Aspen's offices either, though her documents were notarized there.

I asked five of Aspen's notaries if I could examine their journals. I was anxious to see what identifying information they'd recorded for those two investors.

Katy Wadhams Spanish is the daughter of local attorney and lobbyist Jim Wadhams and his wife Colleen, who is a member of the Quinn/Guinn/Sartini prayer group. Colleen and I have been acquaintances for years. Katy Wadhams Spanish had the misfortune of working for Aspen as a notary. When I called Katy about her work as an Aspen notary, she admitted she "did what I was told to do" at Aspen. That was before her father, the attorney, told her to stop talking.

Retired from Aspen and caring for young children when I called her, Katy Wadhams Spanish said she did not have her notary book, which she was required by law to keep for seven years. She invoked the Fifth Amendment right against self-incrimination at her deposition in the Ruthe case.

Linda Millican was another former notary at Aspen who told me she couldn't find her notary book. Then she stopped taking my calls. Millican swore under oath numerous times as a notary that Aspen investor Mary Ann Arminio appeared before her to execute documents. Arminio testified in 2012 that she's never met Millican.

Q: Below it is a notary block. And it says, "This instrument was acknowledged before me March 25, 2008, by Mary Ann Arminio," and then there's a name of Linda Millican. That's the notary. Do you see that?
A: I see that.
Q: You did not appear in front of Linda Millican on March 25, 2008?
A: There's no way I could have. This is my first trip back to Nevada since I moved to Oregon.
Q: So this document is false on its face that you appeared in front of Linda Millican on March 25, 2008. Correct?
MR. LIEBMAN: Object as to form.
THE WITNESS: Correct.
BY MR. PRINCE:
Q: So you would have signed this, mailed it in, and someone would have notarized it at some point later. Correct?
A: Correct.
Q: Do you even know Linda Millican?
A: No.
BY MR. PRINCE:

Q: Let me hand you Exhibit 2, which is another Special Power of Attorney for Canyons Promenade, LLC. Is that your signature on the second page?

A: That's my signature.

Q: The document, according to the date above your signature, is January 7, 2008. Do you see that?

A: I see that.

Q: You would have signed this while in Oregon. Correct?

A: Yes.

Q: Again, it is notarized by Linda M. Millican. It says that you acknowledge the instrument before her on January 7, 2008. Is that accurate?

A: I wasn't in front of Ms. Millican to sign this.

Q: So you did not sign this in front of her. Correct?

A: I did not sign it in front of her.

Q: You didn't sign her notary book, did you?

A: I did not sign her notary book.

Q: You didn't provide her with your identification identifying this is you who was signing this?

A: No, I did not.

Q: So she must have notarized it obviously after you sent it back to Aspen. Correct?

A: Correct.

BY MR. PRINCE:

Q: Handing you Exhibit 3, which is another Special Power of Attorney for the Golshan Weber loan of $9,890,000. Is that your signature on the second page?

A: That's my signature.

Q: You dated it with your own handwriting March 3, 2007?

A: Correct.

Q: And there's the notary block on the bottom of the page that indicates that you acknowledged the document before Linda Millican on March 3, 2007. Is that accurate?

A: It's not accurate because I wasn't in front of her.

Q: Is it your testimony that you never signed any document in front of

Linda Millican at any time?
A: No, I have not ever signed anything in front of her.
Q: Handing you now what's Exhibit 4, which is a Special Power of Attorney for Desert Land, LLC. Is that your signature on the second page?
A: Yes, that's my signature.
Q: The date above your signature is August 6, 2007?
A: Yes, that's my date. Yes.
Q: And Ms. Millican is again notarizing the document stating that the instrument was acknowledged before her on August 6, 2007. Is that accurate by Ms. Millican?
A: That is not accurate.
Q: Because you did not appear before her on August 6. 2007. Correct?
A: I did not appear in front of her.
BY MR. PRINCE:
Q: This is another, Exhibit 5 is another Special Power of Attorney for the Grand Teton Residential, LLC loan. Is that your signature on the second page?
A: Yes, it is.
Q: According to this the date above your signature is May 9, 2007. Do you see that?
A: I see that.
Q Again, on the second page of the document, Ms. Millican is notarizing as a notarial officer of the state of Nevada that the instrument was acknowledged before her on May 9, 2007. Is that accurate?
A: It's not accurate. I wasn't present to sign this in front of her.
Q: So her statement is, her acknowledgment is false. Correct?
A: Correct.[81]

Five notaries and not one journal. Nevada law (NRS 240.147) prohibits

---

[81] Mary Ann Arminio deposition p. 28/29 August 16, 2012

a person from knowingly destroying, defacing, or concealing a notary record.

NRS 240.150 allows the Secretary of State to assess a $2,000 civil penalty for each violation. Secretary of State Ross Miller assessed that penalty against two of Guinn's notaries: Linda Millican and Katy Wadhams Spanish.

The law also allows the Secretary of State to fine and hold the employer liable for damages *"proximately caused by the misconduct of the notary public, if:*

(a) The notary public was acting within the scope of his or her employment at the time the notary public engaged in the misconduct; and
(b) The employer of the notary public consented to the misconduct of the notary public."

Secretary of State Ross Miller had the authority to go after Jeff Guinn for appearing to have orchestrated the Great Notary Journal Disappearance. I fully expected he would.

61: THE SHORT

The FBI heard again in March of 2012 from Helen Peabody, the woman from Visalia, California who put much of her retirement with Aspen.

Peabody wrote that Aspen wanted to pay fifty cents on the dollar in exchange for her shares and release of any claim on Building F at 710 Coronado Center Drive, owned by Aspen President Jeff Guinn. "Complainant believes that _____ is, in essence, trying to create his own short sale."

62: All the Governors' Sons

On March 15, 2012, the FBI's White-Collar Crime program in Las Vegas contacted the Nevada Secretary of State's office for a possible joint investigation of Jeff Guinn. The FBI file contains no further mention of the Secretary of State, and no indication as to whether the agencies collaborated.

Back in 2012, Ross Miller was looking ahead to the 2014 election and to becoming Attorney General. The last thing he needed was to complicate the process with an investigation of Jeff Guinn, who, like Miller, was the son of a former Nevada governor.

The Secretary of State was popular, a handsome family man and a rising star in the Nevada Democratic Party. Miller also had a penchant for the spotlight, including Ultimate Fighting and other big events, to which he accepted thousands of dollars in comps he attempted to describe as related to his profession.

When the son of another Nevada Governor, Mike O'Callaghan, who was named for his famous father, applied for a job as the city attorney of Henderson, but got edged out by Josh Reid, one of Harry Reid's sons, Miller gave O'Callaghan a job. O'Callaghan, a former assistant district attorney, went to work as an investigator for Miller, the Secretary of State.

O'Callaghan was assigned the notary investigation involving Jeff Guinn, but unlike his famous father—both governor and newsman—this Mike didn't dig too deep.

O'Callaghan telephoned Mary Ann Arminio, one of the Aspen investors who told me her documents were notarized by Aspen after she returned them by mail, which is a violation of law.

The Anointed Son

Strangely, Arminio told me O'Callaghan seemed more interested in my actions than Jeff Guinn's.

O'Callaghan, according to Arminio, asked if "Dana Gentry has anything fishy going on," and whether I was laying all my cards on the table!

Mrs. Arminio didn't know what to make of the conversation. Neither did I. I phoned Mike O'Callaghan. He answered.

"Hi Mr. O'Callaghan, this is Dana Gentry. I just spoke with a source who says you called her under the auspices of investigating Jeff Guinn but ended up asking about me."

Click.

I called back. No answer. I called again. No answer. Again. No answer.

It was a freaking brethren! Guinn, Miller, O'Callaghan—all part of the same, elite circle. The Sons of Nevada Governors. All the Governors' Sons, as one of my more creative friends put it. I sighed. Loudly. I'm not the gambling type, but I would have taken bets at that point that the Secretary of State, tasked with ensuring compliance among Nevada notaries, would be taking no action against Jeff Guinn. And I would have won.

On June 4, 2012, I wrote the following on my Las Vegas Sun blog:

Secretary of State Ross Miller fines former Aspen Financial notaries for "losing" journals. Aspen's Jeff Guinn asking court for protective order to keep journals confidential. Why, when they are already "lost"?

Waiting to hear from Miller on whether notaries are skating on allegations they executed documents outside presence of signer.

In the end, Miller fined the notaries $2000, and took no action against Jeff Guinn for, in all likelihood, orchestrating the Flight of the Notary Journals.

63: THE SUN SHINES (BRIEFLY)

Brian Greenspun may not have understood the journalistic issues at stake in Aspen's efforts to gain information about me. But his editorial staff got it.

My employer, the Las Vegas Sun, had not yet signed on to the Amicus Brief in support of my Supreme Court case. Nevertheless, the paper penned an editorial in my support in April of 2012.

I was grateful for the Sun's support, despite Brian Greenspun's unholy alliance with the Guinn camp. My gratitude would rapidly fade.

64: THE FINAL TAKE

In January of 2008, I began writing a blog for the Las Vegas Sun called *The Final Take*. It was initially a place for my musings about producing *Face to Face*, anecdotes about guests, and happenings behind the scenes. With the help of Sun Managing Editor Mike Kelley, who took it upon himself to edit my blog, *The Final Take* quickly became a place for news. Kelley, feared and disliked by some in the Sun newsroom, was a mensch to me. When Jon Ralston protested that voicing my opinions could be problematic for the program, Kelley disagreed and told me to keep writing.

Kelley left the Sun at the end of 2009. Ralston, who took over editing my blog for its final two and a half years, proved to also be an excellent editor.

In July 2012, an Aspen employee testified in deposition that the FBI had subpoenaed a former Aspen employee to appear before a Federal Grand Jury. Here's how I reported it on my blog on the Las Vegas Sun website.

Tuesday, July 24, 2012 | 10:10 a.m.

A former employee of Jeff Guinn, the son of former Governor Kenny Guinn, has been subpoenaed to appear before a federal grand jury investigating Guinn and his hard-money lending company Aspen Financial. That's just one of the startling revelations contained in the deposition of loan counselor and longtime Aspen Financial employee Tania Steffora.

Guinn is being sued by investors who claim he defrauded them of millions of dollars.

Steffora, who was represented at a July 9 deposition in a civil lawsuit by criminal attorney Dan Albregts, says in June the Justice Department delivered a subpoena to former Aspen employee Irma Andrade. Andrade, Steffora says, turned the subpoena over to Guinn who directed her to Albregts.

Steffora, who told attorneys she was a cocktail waitress and convention worker before becoming Guinn's personal assistant in 1999, said at one time she and her father held $3 million in Aspen investments. Steffora said she had no training in what state law required of hard money lenders and acknowledged Aspen routinely ignored state law requiring that investors sign disclosure documents before depositing money. Guinn, she says, told state regulators it was "virtually impossible" to comply with the law and "they understood." Aspen Financial has received high ratings from the state's Mortgage Lending Division. Guinn and his attorney John Bailey did not respond to requests for comment.

Steffora said she often solicited investments for loans secured by property for which she had no appraisal, and provided varying degrees of disclosure to potential investors, depending on who they were.

On Friday, Clark County District Judge Allan Earl rejected Guinn's efforts to seal court documents in a civil case revealing Aspen Financial V.P. Elaine Elliott received a target letter from the U.S. Justice Department. Sources say such a letter amounts to an intent to indict.

To say the blog hit a nerve with someone is an understatement. It was the last item I would write for the Las Vegas Sun.

The next day, I was taken off the story because publisher Brian Greenspun and editor Tom Gorman said I had become part of it. Ironically, just three months earlier, Gorman had written the editorial in the Sun supporting me. My bosses at the Sun had done what Guinn and company had tried to do for so long—killed the story, at least in the Sun.

With a Supreme Court case pending, the timing couldn't have been worse. Once again, the thought of getting off the story never occurred to me as an option. It was complicated, and not the kind of story a reporter could quickly absorb. I told Jon I had no choice but to quit.

Within days, I submitted my resignation. Ralston, who was having his own issues with Greenspun, also quit. We were already producing our programs at the NBC affiliate in Las Vegas, KSNV. Thanks to station owner Jim Rogers, we would now become official employees.

A month later, the newspapers reported our departure, why I was leaving, and speculation as to whether Jon walked in solidarity. He had, partially, but Jon had his own good reason.

Brian Greenspun had scrapped a column Jon wrote that was critical of Harry Reid's attempted shakedown of Mitt Romney over his tax returns. He vowed never again to write a column for the Sun.

Despite assurances from Greenspun and Gorman that another reporter would pick up the Aspen story, the Sun has not published a word about Jeff Guinn since my departure.

65: THE INVESTMENT MANAGER

Tania Steffora is a former cocktail waitress who testified in litigation against her boss, Jeff Guinn, that she went to work at the Las Vegas Convention and Visitors Authority, where she met Monica Guinn, who also worked at the LVCVA at the time.

Steffora eventually joined the staff at Aspen Financial Services as an administrative assistant and moved up to investment manager. It proved to be a highly profitable job for Steffora, not just in salary and commissions, but in trust deed investments as well. Steffora testified at one time that she and her father had $3 million invested in Aspen loans. In fact, a number of Aspen employees held surprisingly large stakes in the deals the company brokered.

When Aspen Financial Services had a loan to sell, Tania Steffora knew how to raise the necessary funds from lenders. She talked about it under oath on July 9, 2012, and about how she came to be represented by criminal attorney Dan Albregts. Steffora said she was given a number to call by Aspen Vice President Sean Corrigan.

Prince: Did you ask him any questions?
Steffora: No
Q: So you didn't think to ask him, "Sean, why are you giving me a criminal defense lawyer's number? Why would I need that?"
A: There was some conversation about taking the Fifth.
Q: About who taking the Fifth?
A: Me.[82]

The Ruthes' attorney, Dennis Prince, asked Steffora about the FBI

---

[82] Tania Steffora deposition July 9, 2012 p. 14

contacting former Aspen employee Irma Andrade.

Q: What did she tell you?
A: That she had been contacted – somebody served her something at home. She was in Hawaii. Her husband accepted it. Conrad. Somebody from Conrad's office.
Q: Okay. Who is Conrad?
A: Somebody with FBI or something that's been involved in all this. ...
Q: Did you tell Jeff Guinn that she called you?
A: Yes, I did.
Q: What did he tell you?
A: He told me to have her call–to call the attorneys or something and have her call Mr. Albregts. [83]

Prince asked Steffora about her own investments–and how many loans she's invested in.

A: Maybe 20 to 25. I don't know.
Q: Totaling how much?
A: At one time it was 3 million. With my dad's and mine. Approximately.
Q: Of monies actually invested?
A: Yes.
Q: And how many loans does your father have?
A: Probably somewhere about the same. [84]

Steffora, who served as manager of Aspen's Investment Department, was unaware of what services Aspen Financial Services provided.

Q: How long have you held that position?
A: Since 2005 or six. ...
Q: Do you know what a mortgage broker is?
A: Well, they would broker loans, yes.

---

[83] Steffora p. 19
[84] Steffora P. 38

Q: Is Aspen a mortgage broker to your knowledge?
A: We fund loans. We're a servicer.
Q: You're a servicer?
A: Yes.
Q: Okay. Would you consider Aspen a mortgage broker as you understand it?
A: Well, no. I mean we service loans. We put a borrower and lenders together. Fund the loan and then get it serviced through the duration. [85]

Aspen Financial Services was a licensed mortgage broker.

Q: Okay. Did anyone from Aspen ever provide you any training as it relates to the disclosure laws applicable to these types of investments required under Nevada law?
A: Disclosure laws?
Q: Right.
A: No. Disclosure laws, no.
Q: Did anybody ever tell you or explain to you what needs to be disclosed to an investor before Aspen takes in any money from that investor?
A: Yes. The particulars of the loan.
Q: Okay. And who provided you that training?
A: It's not training. It's written there on the paper. ... [86]
The person would say, "Yes, I'm interested in this loan. I'm pledging $10,000." So they would send their check in. They would come by the office. At one point, we would generate documents. And if they had any other questions, they could review them at that time. ... [87]
Q: Okay. Now, how were you compensated when you became an investment counselor?
A: My salary earned and commission.
Q: Okay. But what sort of commission were you given?

---

[85] Steffora p. 54

[86] Steffora p. 62

[87] Steffora p. 66

A: It was a basis point.
Q: One basis point?
A: Basis point breakdown. I don't remember it.
Q: Okay. And so how would it—how would it work?
A: Based on the investors you got. The total amount of investors that you got—you got—that was calibrated out. I don't—I can't explain it. It was a calculation of how much money you raised.
Q: Okay. So let's just say a loan is a million dollars.
A: Uh-huh.
Q: And you raised a million dollars. How would you be compensated on a commission basis?
A: I don't have that information in front of me, and I don't remember it.
Q: What's your best estimate?
A: I don't have a best estimate. I can't come up with a number.
Q: You're telling me that as you sit here today, you want this jury to believe that you couldn't tell us, even an estimate, of how much commission you would receive assuming you raised a million dollars in the early 2000 timeframe?
A: No, I can't. ....[88]
Q: Did you ever receive any training by anyone from Aspen concerning the requirements of a mortgage broker's disclosure pursuant to NRS Chapter 645?
A: Any training—rephrase. Say that again.
Q: Did you receive any training by Aspen concerning the disclosure requirements under Nevada law NRS Chapter 645.
A: No. I received no—there was no class training, no.
Q: Okay. Was there any type of even informal training concerning those requirements?
A: Not that I recall.
Q: Are you familiar with Chapter 645 of the Nevada Revised Statutes concerning—applicable to investment brokers?
A: Not off the top of my head, no
Q: Have you ever reviewed any statutory provision concerning

---

[88]Steffora p. 69

disclosures that a mortgage broker must give an investor.
A: Yes. I probably have.
Q: Okay. And do you know what those requirements are?
A: No. Not off the top of my head. ...[89]
Q: Did Aspen have a custom and practice to send the investor any disclosure documents or an opening package before the check would be sent in?
A: If they requested it, yes.
Q: If they didn't request it—let's assume they didn't request it.
A: If they didn't request it, they got their documents with the opening package at funding.
Q: Okay. And so they would get their opening package after the loan funded; correct?
A: Because that's when it closed, yes.
Q: All right. So they would get their opening package sometime after the closing; correct?
A: The complete opening package with documents would come within a day or two after the closing, yes.
Q: Who at Aspen is the person responsible for establishing when the opening package is sent to an investor?
MR. LIEBMAN: Don't answer.
Asked and answered.[90]

Steffora testified that her disclosures to investors depended largely on what they asked, rather than a consistent practice of disclosing certain elements.

Q: Would you tell them—without an investor having to ask you, would you tell them that this loan has interest reserve in it?
A: I may, I may not.
Q: Okay.
A: Depends on the client.

---

[89] Steffora p. 75
[90] Steffora p. 114

Q: What would it depend upon?
A: It would depend upon the client, what questions are asked of me regarding what loans I had.
Q: So I guess whether you told an investor there was interest reserve on a particular loan would be based upon questions from the client to you?
A: There may or may not be.
Q: So your typical presentation to an investor between 2002 and 2007 would not be to initially inform them there would be interest reserve for the loan.
A: It depends on the loan.
Q: What would it depend upon?
A: I don't know. It would depend on me talking to them and going through the thing. I may or may not mention it. It's an individual basis.[91]

Put aside for a moment the tortured logic that only some investors are entitled to essential information. The bigger problem was that Aspen Financial routinely mailed out disclosure documents only after the loans had closed.

Availing potential investors of that information before the fact would likely have rapidly eroded Aspen's list of lenders, and Guinn likely knew it. Unlike other hard money lenders, Aspen never adopted the practice of posting salient loan information on the internet, where it would have been available to all.

Dennis Prince went on to ask Aspen's investment manager, Tania Steffora, about the broker's compliance with Nevada disclosure laws designed to protect investors.

Q: Let's look at this document that's Exhibit 3. Do you know what this is?
A: Yes.
Q: What is it?

---

[91] Steffora p. 131-132

A: These are the lender documents that are signed by the investor. ...
Q: It says "Pursuant to NRS 645B. 185, each investor must sign and date a disclosure form before a mortgage broker or mortgage agent accepts money for the investment.

This form must be executed for each separate loan in which the investor invests money.

A mortgage broker or mortgage agent may not act as the investor's attorney-in-fact or agent in the signing or dating of this form and may not by agreement alter or waive any of these disclosure requirements." Did I read that correctly?
A: Yes.
Q: And why did Aspen violate that law by accepting money before this disclosure document was signed?
A: Because these documents weren't available. They could have been available at the date if we had all the information to print on this.
Q: Well, why didn't you have the investors come in to sign these disclosure documents before you accepted the money?
A: Because that wasn't always an option with some of our investors.
Q: Well, it says right—well, but the law mandated that of you as—
A: I think we had discussed this issue with the mortgage lending division.
Q: Who did?
A: Jeff Guinn. [92]

Steffora testified that she often sold interest in loans to investors without having an appraisal in hand.

A: They've got this whole—they have everything right here. I'm selling a loan, saying "These are the facts that I have." Right here you have an appraised value. It doesn't mean I have to wait for an appraisal to sell it. If you don't—if you feel uncomfortable and "Oh, I don't like this loan because you don't have an appraisal," then wait until I do get the

---

[92] Steffora p. 131-132

appraisal. ...
Q: ...do you believe it's reasonable for an investor to rely upon your representations as to the nature and terms of the loan?
A: Yes.
Q: Okay. Because the vast majority of the time, it was a verbal presentation of the loan; correct?
A: Yes.
Q: And the vast majority of the time you did not send any investors any documents or any information; correct?
A: no.
Q: I'm correct?
A: Yes.[93]

Steffora said most investors simply understood that loan payments were impounded through interest reserves—in other words, that lenders were loaning the borrower the money to make the payments.

Q: All right. But my question is would you explain to the seller–or excuse me, the investor that a portion of it, if it's a second, that a portion of these loan proceeds are going to be interest reserve for a–
A: I may have, depending on who I am talking to.
Q: Why would it depend on who you're talking to? Why wouldn't you make it the same for every investor?
A: I don't know. I can't say that I did or I didn't because I can't remember my conversations about the loans.
Q: Okay. And so is it saying that your level of disclosure would vary between each individual investor?
A: At some times, yes.[94] ...

That revelation should be of great comfort to the thousands of investors who failed to benefit from Steffora's selective disclosure of information and lost their money.

---

[93]Steffora p. 144
[94]Steffora p. 149

Former Aspen executive David Moody testified in deposition why it's improper to create a loan to fund payments on another loan.

Q: Let's assume that Aspen arranges for or obtains a loan for a first trust deed in the amount of $10 million. Okay? And then at some point later obtains a second deed of trust for $5 million that in part funds interest reserve for the first trust deed. Okay?
And then after placing the second on there, refinances the first in its entirety, and now the new first—it now has, say $12 million that's its loan amount. Did you ever see that happen?
A: No
Q: I mean if you saw that happen, would you be concerned about it?
A: Yes.
Q: For the same reason as I stated before. It would eat away at the equity.[95]

Dennis Prince went on to ask Steffora about Aspen's "good borrowers."

Q: Do you ever remember representing that any borrower made all their payments on time and was a repeat borrower?
A: Yes, we had many repeat borrowers and the interest reserve, they made their payments on time. Aspen made their payments on time.
Q: Well, they didn't make their payments on time. Aspen made the payments on time through interest reserve; right?
A: Okay...
Q: Do you feel it was your obligation in order to fully disclose the terms of the loan that where was going to be full interest reserve or even a partial interest reserve, you should explain that to the investor?
A: I would say sometimes I did. I can't remember any conversation yes or no. I mean if it came up in conversation, yes. Was it part of like a bullet list? No.[96]

---

[95] Steffora p. 59
[96] Steffora p. 154

The Anointed Son

Prince asked Steffora if she notified potential investors on how loan proceeds would be used.

> Q: So this is an existing mini storage of some type. $930,000 of the proceeds are going to go to pay off an existing mortgage. Borrower is going to take out a million dollars. That's almost—it's more than 90 percent of the loan proceeds. Did you tell the borrowers (I believe he meant "lenders") that, that the vast majority of the money is not going to the project?
> A: I didn't see this paper, so I might not have—I didn't have this information to convey to anybody. Was it relevant for me to sell the loan? I don't know. I don't—I didn't have this.
> Q: So really like—so not one penny is going to go towards this project; right? I mean using this use of fund—
> A: I have no comment on this paper because it came from the loan department.
> Q: Well, I'm asking you. I'm asking you.
> A: I don't know. [97]
>
> ...
>
> Q: "The proceeds of the indebtedness advanced by the beneficiary and evidenced by the note are to be used only for the purposes of acquiring the property and reimbursement of capital improvements made to the property." What steps did you take as the investment counselor to the Ruthes to make sure that the borrower could only use the money... to acquire the property or reimburse for capital improvements?
> A: Like I said, this is not a document that I would do or have been doing nor did I get that—those are not questions for me or that I can answer. [98]

---

[97] Steffora p. 162
[98] Steffora p. 164

66: Monica Guinn Deposed

"I think during the time that Jeff was, during his time of use when he was taking narcotics, he wasn't the nicest person." —Monica Guinn, August 2012 deposition, Ruthe v. Guinn

The long-awaited deposition of Jeff Guinn's wife, Monica, took place in August of 2012.

Donna and Chuck Ruthe's attorney, Dennis Prince, began by asking Mrs. Guinn about her husband's relationship with Steve Quinn.

A: It was a business relationship, and their friendship fell apart.
Q: So once the business relationship fell apart between Mr. Quinn and your husband, then you stopped being friends with both Steve and his wife?
A: No, it goes a little deeper than that.
Q: How is it deeper than that:
A: Well, they had also a relationship that was not only a business relationship, but they partied together.
Q: Who partied together?
A: My husband and Steve Quinn.
Q: When you say they partied together, what do you mean by that?
A: They took drugs together.
Q: Okay, what type of drugs?
A: Lortab.
Q: Okay. And when was that?
A: That was over seven years ago.
Q: Okay. And so it was before or after your husband got out of rehab

that they took drugs together?
A: Obviously, it was before my husband went to rehab.
Q: Why is it obvious?
A: Once, because once my husband went to rehab, he no longer took Lortab after that.
Q: Okay.
A: He, my husband decided to become a man, went to rehab. Once he went to rehab, he no longer took pain pills after that. And he's been clean and sober for seven years.
Q: Okay. And so, but how does that relate to Steve Quinn then?
A: Because once you go into rehab, you can no longer associate yourself with people who use.
Q: Okay. And so once your husband got out of rehab, did you tell your husband or encourage your husband not to associate with Steve Quinn?
A: No, that was a choice that he made.
Q: He made that choice. Did you support that choice?
A: Of course.
Q: And so he made a choice after he got out of rehab to disassociate himself with Steve Quinn?
A: Well, that and the combination of the construction defect lawsuit and the judgment. So that whole relationship and the combination with the no longer being able to be a friendship over the drug use. [99] ...

Under oath in 2012, Monica Guinn testified about the odd places she'd find her husband's pills before he entered recovery.

Q: Did you find them everywhere?
A: No, in a few spots.
Q: Where would you find them at?
A: Shoes. [100]

Donna Ruthe testified in 2008 in Steve Quinn's defamation case against

---

[99] Monica Guinn deposition p. 17-18
[100] Monica Guinn p. 123

Jeff Guinn that Vicki Quinn helped Monica Guinn clear the Guinn home of drugs.

Donna Ruthe: Monica said he was using some of-- actually having filling prescriptions she would get, and he was using some of hers. So I do remember that.
Q: So it was your understanding from Monica directly that she had prescriptions for certain types of pain medication—
A: I have no idea.
Q: —and that Jeff would take hers?
A: Yes. But Jeff also admitted to that, too.
Q: To you?
A: Yes. When he said everything. He was talking about what he did do.
Q: What else did he tell you about in terms of the drugs that he did do? Did he tell you how bad the habit was or how much he was taking during a day?
A: Yes.
Q: What did he say to you?
A: Well, he would take them morning, noon, and night. And I don't know if the figure was something they were joking about, but they said somewhere between 70 different kinds of pills.
Q: Per day?
A: Yes. And I don't—I don't know if it was a sarcastic remark or...
Q: Who said that to you? Him?
A: Him and Monica in conversations. Because after—she shared with me that her friendship with Vicki, when Jeff went away, Vicki helped her go through the whole house to clean everything out and find everything that Jeff had pertaining to the drugs, where they were hidden in shoes, closets, et cetera. She was just sharing that.
Q: Monica said that Vicki Quinn came over to her home and helped her, I guess for lack of a better word, do a sweep of where all the drugs were hidden—
A: Yes. Because I think—
Q: —and remove them?

A: —she said that Steve took Jeff and brought him to the rehab.[101]

The Ruthes' attorney, Dennis Prince, questioned Monica Guinn about the extent of Quinn's involvement in Jeff Guinn's drug use.

Q: You stated yesterday that Steve Quinn and your husband partied with one another. And I would like to avoid using vernacular phrases, and I would like you to define for me with some precision what you meant by that.
Partying can mean a number of things to different people. It could mean going out to clubs. It could mean going out dancing. It could be going to see movies.
Define for me what you meant when you articulated yesterday that Steve Quinn and your husband partied with one another?
A: Well, I think they had some use together. They both used Lortab together.
Q: Okay. Did they use that for recreational purposes?
A: I can't answer that for you.
Q: Okay. How often would this activity occur?
A: I can't, also cannot answer that for you. That I don't know.
Q: Okay. Other than unspecified use, which you don't know when or how often it occurred, can you give me any more information about partying that took place between your husband and Stephen Quinn?
A: No, I can't.[102] ...
Q: Do you blame Mr. Quinn for your husband's drug problem?
A: No.
Q: Okay. Does your husband blame Mr. Quinn for his drug problems?
MR LIEBMAN: Objection. Calls for speculation. To the extent you learned that information through communication with your husband, don't respond. If you learned it through someone else, you can respond.
A: I'm not going to answer.
Q: Are you aware if this drug issue is the impetus or motivation for

---

[101] Donna Ruthe deposition 2008 Page 112
[102] Monica Guinn p. 249 – 250

litigation against the Quinns?
A: No.
Q: No, it's not; or no, you're not aware?
A: No, it's not. ...
Q: Have you ever heard or suggested that your husband, Jeff Guinn, has ever acted to harm or ruin something–somebody?
A: No.
Q: Do you have any information to support or suggest that the reason for the countersuit in the Precision Construction matter was to ruin or harm the Quinns?
A: No.
Q: To punish them in any way?
A: No.
Q: Do you have any information or knowledge to suggest that the countersuit in this case was filed for the purposes of ruining or harming the Quinns?
A: No. ...
Q: Do you have any information at all or whether or not the Quinns ever funneled any money towards a public smear campaign against Jeff Guinn?
A: No.
Q: Do you have any information at all that the Quinns ever authored any correspondence in support of a public smear campaign against Jeff Guinn?
A: No.
Q: Okay. Do you have any information or knowledge as to whether the Quinns forwarded any emails or documents in support of a public smear campaign against Jeff Guinn.
A: No, I don't.
Q: Do you have any information or knowledge as to whether the Quinns spoke to any persons in advancement of a public smear campaign against Jeff Guinn?
A: Any person? No.
Q: Do you have any information at all that they abetted in the commission of a public smear campaign against Jeff Guinn?

A: No.
Q: You do know who Dana Gentry is. Correct?
A; Yes.
Q: Do you know her from the television, or do you have a personal relationship with her?
A: I met her through Vicki Quinn. ...
Q: Do you have any information at all which would support or suggest that the Quinns dictated or directed what Dana Gentry broadcast on her television show?
Mr. Liebman: Object as to form. You can respond.
A: Not personally, no.
Q: Do you harbor a belief that the Quinns dictated or directed what Dana Gentry broadcast on her television show?
A: Yes, somewhat, I do.
Q: Okay. Is that a hunch or speculation on your part, or can you articulate for me any facts which would support—
A: It's a hunch.
Q: Okay. Do you have any reason to believe that Dana Gentry is anything other than a fair and honest reporter? ...
A: I do not think she's a fair reporter.
Q: Okay. And again, is that just a hunch, or something you know in your heart, or can you articulate for me any facts—
A: That's a hunch.[103] ...
Q: Did you ever witness Jeff Guinn, or overhear Jeff Guinn telephoning Dana Gentry for any reason or purpose?
A: I know they spoke on the phone.
Q: Do you know for what reason or purpose?
A: No, I wasn't witness to their conversations.
Q: Okay. Do you know if it had anything to do with Mike Shustek?
A: I don't, I don't know what their conversations were about. [104]
Q: Do you have any information regarding whether Dana Gentry, Stephen Quinn, and Vicki Quinn helped Donna investigate and prepare

---

[103] Monica Guinn p. 264

[104] Monica Guinn p. 284

this lawsuit?
A: No, I don't. But I would imagine they probably all worked on it together.
Q: Why? Why do you imagine that?
A: Just a general feeling.
Q: Nothing more than a general feeling?
A: No.[105] ...
Q: Now, have you ever heard Jeff ever say that he wants—or have you ever heard Jeff tell someone, tell another person that he wanted to destroy Kevin Donahoe?
A: Not that I can remember.
Q: Have you ever heard Jeff tell anyone he wanted to harm, ruin, or destroy Kit Graski?
A: Not that I can remember.
Q: Did you ever hear Jeff overtell anyone that he wanted to harm, hurt, or destroy Stephen Quinn?
A: Not that I can remember.
Q: Have you ever heard Jeff say to anyone that he wanted to harm, hurt, or destroy Donna or Chuck Ruthe?
A: Not that I can remember.
Q: Have you ever heard Jeff tell anyone that he wanted to harm, hurt or destroy Michael Shustek, who owns Vestin Mortgage?
A: No.
Q: Now, have you ever, were you ever present in the office when Jeff made telephone calls to Dana Gentry?
A: No, not that I can remember. I know that he called her, but I never sat in the office when he spoke to her.
Q: In fact, there was a period of time before this lawsuit involving the Ruthes that he called Dana frequently. Right?
A: I don't know how frequently he called her.
Q: But he did call her more than once, right?
A: I don't know how often he called her.
Q: In fact, he would call her, to your knowledge, about Michael Shustek

---

[105] Monica Guinn p. 306

and Vestin Mortgage. That's the reason why he was calling her. Right?
A: I have no idea how much he called her or what he called her about.
Q: So she wasn't always an enemy of Jeff's. Right?
MR. LIEBMAN: Objection. Calls for speculation. You can respond.
A: No, she was not always an enemy.
Q: In fact, there is a period of time where he spoke highly of Dana. Right?
A: I guess. I don't know.[106]

Prince questioned Monica Guinn about her husband's allegedly strained relationship with his mother, Dema Guinn.

Q: Did he ever describe that to you?
Mr. Bailey Objects.
Q: Did she ever describe, did Dema ever describe a relationship with Jeff with you?
A: No.
Q: Did you ever, did you ever feel on your own, watching Jeff and Dema have a relationship, that that wasn't a very healthy relationship and she had a negative effect on Jeff emotionally as a child and as an adult?
A: Every mother and child has things to work out, and they worked it out really well.
Q: Did Jeff ever have to go to counseling, to your knowledge, you know, emotional counseling, seek a counselor because of difficulties he had growing up as a child and with his parents?
A: He went to counseling after rehab to go, to get, as a man, went to rehab, and has stayed clean and sober for seven years, and has remained in therapy to keep his recovery in check. And he's done well with that.
Q: Did you ever express to any third party ever that you were concerned about Jeff's abusive nature toward you, verbal or physical, in anyway?
A: I don't recall.
Q: Is it possible you might have told people before Jeff went to rehab

---

[106] Monica Guinn p. 316

that he was verbally abusive toward you?
A: Yeah, I, I really don't, I don't recall. You know, during that time, it was a tough time, I don't recall.
Q: Was Jeff ever verbally or physically abusive towards any of the three children before he went to rehab.
A: I'm sure he had times where he wasn't very nice.
Q: Okay. And who was he not nice to?
A: I don't know. I don't recall.[107]

---

[107] Monica Guinn p. 83-86

67: KEEP YOUR FRIENDS CLOSE

During a second day of deposition, Monica Guinn talked about her husband's decision to file a lawsuit against the Guinns' good friends, the Quinns, and have them surveilled. Monica Guinn also speculated as to why Vicki Quinn fled the comfort and companionship she once relied on from the Stillpoint prayer group.

Dennis Prince: Okay. Would either of those occurrences, the retention of an investigator or the commencement of litigation, be the reason that at least you formulated the belief and understanding that she left the prayer group?
Monica Guinn: At that time, I did not think so. And I don't think they were aware of the private investigator at that time.
Q: Was that something you were keeping from them?
A: That I was keeping from them? No.
Q: Okay. You didn't announce this to either Victoria Quinn that you hired an investigator to follow them, did you?....
A: Oh. No.
Q: Why was that decision made?
A: Because Mr. Quinn had threatened my husband's life, and he felt that it was important to protect his family.
Q: Okay. This threat, when was it made?
A: I don't know the exact date.
Q: How was it made?
A: I, I don't have all the details of that. I just know that that was my husband's decision. And he told me it was to protect—
Guinn's Attorney Joseph Liebman: Don't disclose any communications with your husband.
Q: Do you know if this threat was by a letter?
A: It was a verbal threat.

Q: A verbal threat. Was it before or after your husband was released from rehabilitation?
A: I, I believe it was after, but...
Q: Okay. You mentioned yesterday that after Jeff Guinn left rehab, he terminated contact and communications with Stephen Quinn. So I'm a bit curious as to when or how this threat could have been made if the two men were not in communication. Do you have any information or knowledge as to how that threat was communicated?
A: I don't have any knowledge on that.[108]

---

[108] Monica Guinn p. 244-245

68: THE SUPREMES CHIME IN

Of the three appeals Jeff Guinn filed before the Nevada Supreme Court in 2012, the most critical involved Guinn's attempt to avoid being deposed or forced to invoke his Fifth Amendment right against self-incrimination in civil litigation because of the problems it could cause in the criminal probe.

Jeff Guinn's second defeat of the year before the Nevada Supreme Court arrived with the holidays.

The Supreme Court unanimously rejected a request by Jeff Guinn, son of former Gov. Kenny Guinn, to delay a required deposition in a civil case until the FBI finishes its criminal investigation into whether he defrauded real estate clients. ...

Justices noted many of the plaintiffs are elderly and a stay could prevent them from testifying, and that "there is no way to intelligently predict how long the (FBI) investigation may last, much less whether it will in fact culminate in a criminal prosecution."

-December 6, 2012 Las Vegas Review-Journal

As it turned out, the ruling was moot. The FBI was about to wrap up its probe.

69: OFF THE HOOK

It's hard to imagine how Jeff Guinn endured facing a criminal probe by the Feds, civil suits from investors, and the dismantling of Aspen Financial, as one loan after another stopped performing.

Nevada Title owner Terry Wright, whose company earned thousands of dollars almost every time Aspen Financial closed a loan, testified in June 2013 about his communications with Guinn.

Dennis Prince: Have you ever discussed this case with Jeff?
Terry Wright: Yes.
Q: How many times?
A: Once or twice.
Q: When was the first time?
A: I don't know.
Q: Approximately when?
A: Few years ago, maybe.
Q: Was it on the phone or in person?
A: On the phone.
Q: Did he call you or did you call him?
A: He called me.
Q: To ask you what?
A: I don't remember the conversation. I just generally remember that it was about his issues with the Ruthes. But I don't remember any of the specifics of the conversation.
Q: And what—you have no idea what was discussed?
A: No.
Q: Did he ask you any questions?
A: I don't remember.
Q: When was the next time you spoke to him about this case?
A: I think he called me six or eight months ago to tell me that the FBI

probe had ended, or something along those lines.
Q: What was your reaction to that call?
A: I really didn't care much about the call.
Q: Were you ever contacted by an FBI representative?
A: I was not.
Q: Was anybody at Nevada Title ever contacted by someone from the FBI?
A: Not to my knowledge, but I don't know.
Q: What else was discussed during that conversation where he called to tell you the FBI probe had ended?
A: That was all.
Q: Why would he think you would care?
A: Good question. I don't know.
Q: Did you care? Did you say you didn't care, one way or the other?
A: Quite frankly, I didn't even know there was an FBI probe going on. That's probably why I didn't care. [109]

Why did Jeff Guinn call Terry Wright to tell him the probe was over? Wright was not an investor. Was Guinn concerned the feds would take a close look at the subordination agreements (many signed after the fact) and other documents required to close the multi-beneficiary loans and question how Nevada Title accepted them?

If Wright knew, he wasn't saying.

---

[109] Terry Wright depo p. 40-42

70: FEDS TAKE A PASS

In 2012, the U.S. Justice Department considered close to 200,000 prosecutions. Of those, fourteen cases resulted in no indictment. Jeff Guinn's case was one of fourteen.

The timing couldn't have been better for Guinn. It was mid-December, about a week after the State Supreme Court denied Guinn's request to avoid being deposed in the civil cases against him.

Billing records I obtained reveal, and FBI records corroborate, that on December 11, 2012, federal prosecutor turned criminal defense attorney Charles E. Kelly met with the U.S. Attorney's office in Las Vegas. Kelly had been hired by Guinn to represent Aspen Vice President Elaine Elliott. Kelly also met that day with Jeff Guinn's criminal attorney, Richard Wright.

Two days later, Kelly had what he detailed in billing records as "lengthy TCs" (telephone conversations) with Sean Corrigan and Elaine Elliot.

On December 17 and 18, Kelly had conferences with Jeff Guinn and Richard Wright.

A month later, in mid-January of 2013, Guinn's attorneys told the lawyer representing one group of investors that the criminal probe had ended.

In February 2013, the FBI sent letters to Aspen investors informing them the U.S. Attorney's office declined to prosecute the case for lack of evidence.

Today, a decade after the mortgage meltdown that precipitated The Great Recession, the reluctance of the Justice Department to pursue criminal action against questionable actors remains a bitter pill to swallow for countless Americans.

71: The Mouth That Roared

Just as I would have imagined, putting Vicki Quinn on the hot seat generated interesting, if not completely accurate responses.

Aspen Financial and Guinn attorney Joseph Liebman had the pleasure of questioning Vicki under oath in a 2013 deposition.

Q: Did you go to high school with Dana Gentry?
A: I did
Q: Were you good friends then?
A: Absolutely
Q: Are you good friends today?
A: No
Q: Why not?
A: Because she just drives me absolutely crazy.
Q: And when did that begin?
A: A couple years ago.
Q: Anything in particular that caused a rumble in your relationship?
A: Well, you have to understand something and it's important. There's Dana Gentry, the 35-year-old friend that I've had, and there's Dana Gentry, the reporter. If you're talking to Dana Gentry, the friend, which is something like a burden on you or something that you're carrying because you're her friend, it's hard for her not to want to turn it into a story. So I chose a few years ago just to stop talking because it was making me crazy. I wanted to end it and to stop talking about it. And I just didn't want--I just had enough. I'm not emotionally stable about all this. So I needed to eliminate people from my life through counseling, which I'm on, that upset my daily routine, which is someone like Dana.
Q: And this was a few years ago, you said?
A: Yes, now keep in mind, she's been a great friend, but it's hard for her to draw the line between friend and reporter. It's difficult.
Q: Back when you made the decision to kind of limit her from your life, what types of things was she trying to turn into stories when she would

talk to you?
A: You know, I don't even remember if it was about stories. It was about her getting angry and screaming at me. Dana has a hot temper. It wasn't even, Mr. Liebman about stories as just about anything. You know, she just—she's a great friend but she's a difficult person. Does that make sense?[110]

....

Q: Do you know whether or not your husband's company ever performed any work for Dana Gentry?

...

A: No.

Q: What was your involvement with Todd Markwart?

A: Todd has been our employee for many years, and he's like a son to us. He's just a great young man that works for our company.

Q: Ok. Did he do any work on Dana Gentry's house?

A: Yes, he did

Q: And we're you involved in setting that up?

A: Kinda

Q: Okay. How?

A: Well, Dana wanted to redo her bathroom. And I said, you know what, Dana, Todd is out of work. Give him a call, and maybe he can help you. And that was it. I did nothing more. That was it. And she made the arrangements after that.

Q: You don't know what kind of work was done or how the work was paid for or anything like that?

A: I do not.

Q: Your son Paul used to work with Dana Gentry, correct?

A: He did

Q: Was she involved in getting him hired?

A: She was helpful, but basically, she didn't have the authority to get him hired. It was more of Jon wanting to give Paul a chance.

Q: Jon Ralston?

A: Yeah. And giving Paul a chance to work out of college, and it was

---

[110] Vicki Quinn depo p. 35 -37

really nice of them.

Q: Did you ever tell Dana Gentry that you would disclose her drug use unless your son was hired at the company?

A: No

Q: Did you ever make any sort of implied threats in that regard?

A: Well, I just kind of got mad at her one day and screamed at her, but it wasn't about Paul getting hired there. So I do -- it had nothing to do with Paul getting hired.

Q: Were you screaming at her about drug use?

A: No. Just in general.

Q: Okay. Do you know if Ms. Gentry uses drugs?

A: I haven't seen her in a few years. I have no idea what she's doing.

Q: How about back when you did see her?

A: No. I mean, no.

Q: She didn't use any illegal drugs?

A: Well, not in front of me. I don't do drugs, thank God. [111]

---

[111] Vicki Quinn depo p. 42-44

72: MILLER TIME

Ross Miller appeared to be a shoo-in for Attorney General in 2014. As a former prosecutor and the state's current Secretary of State, and with a hankering for high-profile appearances with pop culture up-and-comers, the son of former governor Bob Miller appeared destined to create a Miller Dynasty. The state's highest law enforcement office seemed the next likely step. But enforcing the law is something Miller did selectively as Secretary of State.

In 2012, I reported that notaries at Guinn's Aspen Financial, in violation of state law, notarized investor documents outside the presence of the investor. While it may not seem like a big deal, the practice was an essential element in national mortgage scams involving robo-signing, the fraudulent execution of mortgage documents. It was also a key element of Aspen Financial's business practices.

Investors contend the practice facilitated the alleged fraud perpetrated by Guinn, which they say sometimes involved back-dating documents to appear to be executed before the close of escrow and in compliance with the law. What's more, Aspen's notaries (with one exception) claim they "lost" their notary journals. State law requires the journals be retained for seven years.

Secretary of State Miller fined two of the notaries mentioned in the story for losing their journals, but took no action against Guinn or Aspen, for what appeared to me to have been an orchestrated effort.

In 2013, Donna Ruthe, a frequent contributor to political campaigns, had a conversation with Miller about the then-defunct Aspen Financial and the millions of dollars owed the Ruthes and others for what they say were mortgage-backed investments steeped in fraud.

Ruthe says she relayed to Miller her dissatisfaction with the Secretary

The Anointed Son

of State's failure to sanction Guinn, who Ruthe believes should be held responsible for the failure to produce the journals.

Ruthe says she mentioned to Miller my report on an investor who provided receipts proving she was in New York, not Las Vegas, on days Aspen notaries swore she appeared before them.

In fact, that investor from New York told me she never set foot in Aspen's offices.

Miller, according to Ruthe, said he remembered the story and that the investor, Kimberly Casey, told his investigator she gave Aspen permission to notarize outside her presence.

OK, set aside for a moment the fact that Secretary Miller, according to Ruthe, seemed to be excusing an illegal act. It appeared a correction was in order on my part.

Why, I wondered, would Ms. Casey have changed her story?

Turns out she didn't. In fact, Casey says she was never contacted by Miller's office.

I called Secretary Miller, who told me he couldn't remember what he told Ruthe two weeks earlier, but texted me the number of his securities administrator, Diana Foley, who he said briefed him before his talk with Ruthe.

Ms. Foley first said she had to discuss the matter with Miller. The next day, she phoned to say that under Nevada's confidentiality laws, information obtained in investigations cannot be disclosed.

Hmmm. So, I asked, how could Miller talk with Ruthe? Is the Secretary not bound by the same laws? Yes, but as Foley told me, Ruthe is an interested party.

What, I asked, is an "interested party?" And what law exempts "interested parties" from confidentiality rules? I can't find one. I've asked Miller to inform me, but he has not.

Nor is he saying why he thought it was OK for notaries to "get permission" to execute a document outside the presence of the signer. Here's the email Kimberly Casey's husband sent the FBI:

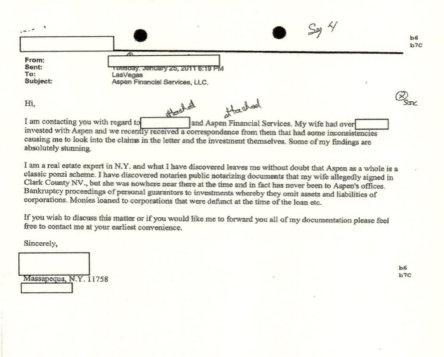

Politics, they say, make for strange bedfellows. In an insular state such as Nevada, the pairings can be downright bizarre.

Among the notables at Democrat Ross Miller's 2013 campaign kickoff for Attorney General was Dema Guinn. The former First Lady, along with another Republican, Dale Raggio, the widow of former Nevada

The Anointed Son

Senate Majority Leader Bill Raggio, would also host a fundraiser for Miller.

Dema Guinn, who had long held the Millers in contempt for the condition in which they left the Governor's Mansion, suddenly displayed a newfound interest in supporting Ross Miller's political career.

73: THE WINDING DOWN

In the end, the Empire that Jeff Built crumbled under the weight of Guinn's own borrowing.

In March of 2013, City National Bank won a judgment of $7.9 million against Aspen Financial as well as Jeff and Monica Guinn. The debt stemmed from three loans with CNB: a $250,000 personal loan taken by Jeff and Monica Guinn in 2007, a $750,000 business loan by Aspen taken at the same time, and a $7.5 million unsecured line of credit taken in July of 2004 that Guinn used to close loans before he sold the interest to individual investors, allowing him to earn the sizable origination fees first.

In April of 2013, the Nevada Mortgage Lending Division determined Aspen was insolvent and in violation of Nevada law. It was the first step toward closing Aspen's doors.

Guinn sent Aspen investors a letter notifying them of the state's action and contending it was his desire to protect them that precipitated the company's downfall.

What Guinn failed to note in that missive to investors: almost one-fifth of Aspen's defaulted $7.5 million line of credit financed just one loan. The borrower: Jeff Guinn.

In his 2013 deposition in the Ruthe case, Guinn contended he was already in the process of "winding down" Aspen Financial. But billing records from Guinn's attorney that I obtained reference conferences after the state's action to discuss the initiation of "winding down" and the potential impact on pending litigation.

Guinn also testified he infused $1.5 million of his own cash in the company in its last three years to keep it afloat.[112]

On April 23, 2013, the same day the Mortgage Lending Division closed Aspen Financial, the MLD's senior examiner, identified by Jeff Guinn in testimony as the person most responsible for Aspen exams, quit his job after more than a decade working for the state agency.

Bill Theobald, who went on to work for All Western Mortgage in Las Vegas as a compliance expert, told me the timing of his departure and Aspen's closure were nothing more than coincidence, noting that he gave notice to the state weeks earlier.

Theobald declined to answer questions about whether his examiners routinely checked to see if disclosure forms were being signed by Aspen investors before money changed hands, as required by law.

---

[112] Jeff Guinn #1 p. 23

74: PAYING THE PIPER

Just days after the state suspended Aspen's mortgage lending license, federal judge Philip Pro confirmed $23 million in judgments in favor of the FDIC (for Community Bank) against Jeff and Monica Guinn, Sean Corrigan, his wife and trusts, and Kent Barry, as well as his wife and trusts.

An FDIC pleading contains this footnote:

The FDIC-R originally asserted claims against the following obligors on the loan: Jeffrey Guinn, Monica Guinn, Mark Brown, Michele Brown, the Jeffrey and Monica Guinn Family Trust, **the Guinn Irrevocable Asset Management Trust 1999***, and the Del Mar Trust. The Guinns filed for bankruptcy protection on October 23, 2013, and Mark Brown filed for bankruptcy protection on March 28, 2014. The United States Bankruptcy Court of the District of Nevada subsequently discharged the Guinns' and Mr. Brown's obligations under this loan.*[113]

In January of 2014, according to federal court records, Jeff Guinn and the FDIC entered into a non-disclosure agreement. Did the agreement eliminate the personal guarantees of Kenny Guinn and the Guinn Irrevocable Asset Management Trust—referred to in federal court documents as the Modified Guarantee?

How did debt secured by Kenny and Dema Guinn's trust get eliminated through Monica and Jeff Guinn's bankruptcy?

---

[113] Doc 310 filed 8/11/14 in FDIC case: **2:09-cv-01809-JAD-CWH**
Footnote: pg 2

Jeff Guinn's attorneys, Bailey and Kennedy, declined to respond, as did attorneys representing the FDIC.

Why the Feds seemingly ignored the personal guarantee of Governor and Mrs. Guinn's trust remains a mystery to this day.

In his 2013 deposition in the Ruthe litigation, Jeff Guinn testified that the FDIC agreed to limit the deficiency on Aspen's office building on West Sahara in Las Vegas, to a maximum of $300,000. The actual deficiency the FDIC claimed on the building, which was owned by a company in which Governor Guinn had an ownership interest was more than $1.3 million.

Why didn't Guinn and Co. come out of pocket to cure their mounting loan defaults?

Here's what Aspen President Sean Corrigan said under questioning by the Ruthes' attorney, Dennis Prince.

Q: And did you or Mr. Guinn have the ability at the time the forbearance was requested to make interest payments to either the first trust deed of 19.5 million or the second trust deed of 2.3 million?
A: During the forbearance? I didn't. I can't speak for Mr. Guinn.
Q: Did you ask Mr. Guinn if he had the ability to do that?
A: No, I didn't.
Q: Why didn't you?
A: I never did.
Q: Why didn't you as the manager go to Mr. Guinn and say, "What's your financial condition? Can you make the payments?"
A: Well, again, as I said, I know he made some payments. I just don't know when that time period was. It may have been during the forbearance. Prior to the forbearance. I'm not sure when it was.

The FDIC, on behalf of Community Bank, won Writs of Execution for more than $9 million against Jeff and Monica Guinn in August of 2013. Two months later, with creditors breathing down their necks and about to execute judgments, Jeff and Monica Guinn filed Chapter 7 bankruptcy, with assets of $451,910 and debts of just under $70 million.

Jeff and Monica Guinn remained cradled in the lap of luxury while discharging millions of dollars in debt through bankruptcy.

2961 Brighton Creek Court in the Las Vegas master planned community known as Summerlin is a one-story home just under 3300 square feet, according to public records. It sold in 2006 at the height of the market for $1.1 million. In June of 2012, former Nevada First Lady Dema Guinn picked it up for about half of that: $610,000. It's where Jeff and Monica Guinn downsized after their Chapter 7 bankruptcy.

Monica Guinn testified in the Ruthe lawsuit about the home just a few months after her mother-in-law bought it.

Attorney Dennis Prince: Now, the house that you're living in on Brighton Creek Court, who is the owner of that house? ...
A: You would have to ask Jeff.
Q: Well, the real property record show that it's a Montreux Trust.
A: So it's, Jeff's mom owns it.
Q: So who paid for the house?
A: We had to borrow the money from Jeff's mom. It's in her trust.
Q: Have you ever, you or Jeff or anyone you directed ever transferred money into the Montreux Trust?
A: No.
Q: Are you supposed to pay her back?
A: No. It's her house. [114]

---

[114] Monica Guinn p. 330

The Anointed Son

Undaunted by the crumbling empire at his feet and the federal criminal probe hanging over his head, Jeff Guinn bought a new Mercedes Benz in August of 2012. Bankruptcy records would later reveal the cost — $77,000 — and the monthly payment — $1300.

Other creditors included Jeff Guinn's criminal attorney, Richard Wright, who Guinn owed $71,500; the IRS, owed $150,000; a deficiency judgment of $2.2 million on the Guinn's property at 10125 Summit Canyon Drive in Las Vegas; about $28.5 million to the FDIC for Community Bank; $850,000 to City National Bank for a line of credit and $9 million for a personal guarantee judgment; a personal guarantee on Coronado Eastern LLC to Guinn's own company, Aspen Financial; and personally guaranteed business debt amounting to $6.5 million.

Jeff and Monica Guinn owed Neiman Marcus and Nordstrom more than $10,000, but claimed only $200 worth of clothing as assets.

Monica Guinn fought to retain jewelry given to her by her husband and children by characterizing the items as "heirloom" pieces. Donna Ruthe, a relentless foe, subpoenaed jewelry purchase records from The Jewelers, M.J. Christensen, and others to prove the rings and other items were newly acquired, not heirlooms, as claimed in the bankruptcy filing.

Jeff and Monica Guinn's son, Colton, would later tell me his parents had him sell expensive watches and other jewelry in order to generate cash and avoid including the items in the bankruptcy.

Colton Guinn also alleges his parents concealed valuable art from the reach of the bankruptcy. The Guinns did not respond to my requests for comment.

While Jeff and Monica Guinn likely hoped the proceedings would allow them to leave their legal troubles behind, it was not to be. The Bankruptcy court granted the Ruthes' petition to proceed with their lawsuit in federal court.

75: LICENSE REVOKED

Aspen Financial Services filed for Chapter 7 bankruptcy protection on June 13, 2013.

The following month, the State of Nevada officially suspended Aspen's license at a revocation hearing.

Neither Jeff Guinn nor his attorney attended the hearing they requested.

Hearing officer Dean Gould deemed Aspen Financial Services a danger to the public, finding the brokerage failed to conduct business in accordance with the law.

Remarkably, Jeff Guinn would attempt a comeback in the hard money lending business.

The Anointed Son

76: Big City, Small Town

Nevada's Supreme Court issues opinions on Thursdays, but on Tuesday, November 26, 2013, the Court's information officer, Bill Gang, sent out a bulletin notifying news organizations that because of the Thanksgiving holiday, opinions would be issued on Wednesday. Among them was the case involving me: Aspen v. District Court (Gentry).

My daughter Chandler, a member of the National Champion UNLV Rebel Girls Dance Team, was performing at the Runnin' Rebel basketball game that Tuesday night. Once in a while, when KSNV owner Jim Rogers wasn't going to a game, he'd offer his second row, center court seats to employees. On that day, I nabbed the tickets and ended up just feet from Chandler as she danced on the floor. Seated next to me was Supreme Court Justice Kris Pickering, a rabid Rebel fan. Pickering was also the only member of the Supreme Court to recuse herself from my case, citing the fact that she knew attorneys involved. During the game, I mentioned the news release announcing the opinions to be filed Wednesday.

"I didn't know if you had heard," Pickering said. "I wasn't going to say anything."

And she said no more.

I have great respect for the network reporters who stand outside the U.S. Supreme Court and somehow make sense of precedent-setting rulings on the fly while on live TV.

On Wednesday, November 27, 2013, I wasn't even on air, but you wouldn't have known it. I refreshed my browser every few minutes, waiting to see if the rulings were out. Jon Ralston was doing the same.

My phone rang at about 10:30 a.m.

"It's out!" Jon said excitedly. "But I can't click on it. The clerk says it will be available in a few minutes."

The status changed on the case docket from "pending" to "petition denied." I was relatively certain that was good, as it was Guinn who filed the petition, not me. I quickly read the caption to the case I had seen so many times. "Petition for a writ of mandamus or prohibition challenging a district court order quashing a subpoena" Yup. We won.

The ruling appeared a few minutes later.

Justice Michael Douglas wrote the opinion, shredding Aspen's contention that they weren't after my sources.

Thankful I was that Thanksgiving to Jon Ralston, our news director Bob Stoldal, then-KSNV General Manager Lisa Howfield, who won the support of the Nevada Broadcasters Association, and journalists George Knapp, Steve Sebelius, and John L. Smith, who wrote columns condemning Guinn and Bailey's tactics. Attorney Mark Hinueber of the Las Vegas Review-Journal didn't know me, but signed on to the effort out of principle and hired attorney Maggie McLetchie to file an amicus' brief.

Most of all, I was and will always remain thankful for Don Campbell. John Bailey may be unscrupulous, but he's a formidable attorney. I don't know many lawyers who could have bested him. I was incredibly fortunate to have one.

Here's how Jon Ralston summed it up in a column on his blog a week after the decision:

I kept saying I never had any doubts how the case would turn out.

But I doubted. And I was afraid.

I knew that what John Bailey, the lawyer for ex-Gov. Kenny Guinn's son,

The Anointed Son

was trying to do was outrageous and unethical and wouldn't be sanctioned in any other profession: Lying in court documents about a journalist's integrity to smear her and chill her reporting. And I firmly believed that the state Supreme Court had opted to consider Bailey's petition for extraordinary relief mostly to squash his methods and perhaps bolster the state's shield law that protects journalists.

I had faith. But I was not sure.

So when I learned the day before Thanksgiving that the high court had not just [eviscerated Bailey and Guinn](), but broadened one of the country's strongest shield laws, I was ecstatic. And relieved.

This was professional, but it was also personal. Very personal.

You see, the journalist who was the victim of Bailey's court calumny is Dana Gentry, one of the more passionate, aggressive reporters I have ever known who also happens to be the producer of "Ralston Reports," my nightly program on NBC affiliates. Excuse me—our nightly program.

To say Gentry and I are close is an understatement. We are professional partners, and she might as well be part of my family. There is no separation; it is always "we."

There seemed to always be an insinuation on the part of the Guinnites and their amen corner that this was "just Dana" pursuing a vendetta, that somehow I was not part of the story. Nothing could be further from the truth, and all of that truth must now be told.

Most of the coverage of the story, that of Guinn being accused of fraud by some of his hard-money lending clients, was on the program that bears my name. Does anyone seriously think I would have allowed Gentry's reporting on the air if I didn't believe in it? (Don't get me started telling stories of some of our knockdown drag outs—it's what makes us such a good team.)

When Gentry is on a story, she has a focus and tenacity that is unmatched. She, like all of us, may make mistakes, but they are never out of malice. I don't even think she understood at the beginning of this ordeal what was at stake, not just for her but for all Nevada journalists, that the precedent that would be set would allow subjects of coverage to scotch reporting by making unsupported accusations and forcing reporters to prove a negative. It was shockingly insidious, and I still believe something no respectable attorney would agree to do for a client.

Gentry immediately wanted to produce the proof that the accusations were false. But I warned her that would only open the door to more obloquy disguised as questions about her relationships and reporting and that we had to fight this all the way. And so we did.

And at the end of that long journey, during which Gentry suffered having those unanswered allegations in the public domain, I learned a lot about some remarkable lawyers, our supportive Fourth Estate colleagues and the righteous justices.

With one glaring exception—Las Vegas Sun Editor Brian Greenspun and his officious toadies -- the media understood what was at stake here and either filed briefs or wrote pieces highlighting Bailey's execrable conduct. And others with no stake in the matter, from political figures to guests on the program to regular folks, backed Gentry, sending encouraging words during the interminable wait for justice.

This is a story of an important legal victory for the business I love, but also one that has heroes who need to be properly recognized and villains who need to be properly vilified.

Five years ago, Gentry began covering the story of how Guinn, while his father was governor, used connections at Metro Police in an attempt to smear his foes in civil litigation. It was foreshadowing of what was to come for her.

The Anointed Son

The story metamorphosed into one of prominent Nevadans alleging that the governor's son had defrauded them. He portrayed their financial losses as part of the vicissitudes of The Great Recession; they saw something more sinister.

It was a great story: Son of former governor sued by big names, with allegations that the Guinn administration had gone soft on hard-money lending. Gentry pursued the story with her usual vigor, never failing to ask Bailey and/or Guinn for a comment before we went on the air.

They never would, nor did they ever challenge any of the facts. Then, suddenly, two and a half years ago, Bailey filed court documents, subpoenaing "information" from Gentry he claimed would prove she had been biased because she had received gifts and favors from plaintiffs suing Guinn.

Even after the high court has put an end to this, I refuse to print the allegations, which could have been easily disproved and would be libelous anywhere but court documents. To this day, I don't know whether Bailey and Guinn knew they were false or simply didn't care. Either way, I can't believe the state Bar countenances such conduct.

Thus began the serpentine road that led to last week's decision, with a District Court judge quashing the subpoena but making <u>some odd statements</u> and then Bailey asking the justices for their extraordinary writ.

Before I get to the decision and what it says and does, I must report that this saga was punctuated by several columns by journalists who realized what was happening. Elizabeth Crum, George Knapp, Steve Sebelius and John L. Smith all penned pieces excoriating Bailey and defending Gentry.

It was gratifying and helpful. We are eternally grateful.

The Sun also <u>published an editorial</u>, but it must be noted that Brian Greenspun, always eager to defend Harry Reid or one of his friends in the paper, never once in all of the years we were employed there (we left a year ago) wrote a column defending Gentry.

But it's much worse than that.

Greenspun, during a conversation I had with him last year in which I asked him to pitch in for the court case, repeatedly told me that he did not understand the principle that was at stake. Indeed, he revealed 15 minutes into the conversation, his attorney was none other than John Bailey and he thought he could get Bailey to provide him questions for Gentry to answer, she could answer them and this would be over.

I was flabbergasted and tried to explain that was out of the question, that it would just open the door to more mischief. Not only did he refuse to write anything helpful or provide any financial backing, but a few months later, Greenspun, aided by his compliant subordinates, yanked Gentry from the story, saying she had a conflict of interest.

In other words, Greenspun did exactly what Bailey, who happened to be his lawyer, and Guinn aimed to do through the courts. Orwell could not have imagined it.

Gentry, of course, was apoplectic and quit soon thereafter. I followed a short time later, after Greenspun killed a column critical of Harry Reid and told me he wanted to still run my column, but wanted KSNV to be my employer. I told him no on the former but happily accepted the latter.

As difficult as that moment was for us, we got past it and Gentry continued to cover the story on her blog and on "Ralston Reports." There was never any question of the station being a backstop, especially with the legendary Bob Stoldal as our boss. No one could ask for a better mentor and defender than Stoldal, who is everything Greenspun was not – loyal, unswerving, tough.

And now the Supreme Court, in that unanimous decision, not only had made it all seem worthwhile but has struck a blow for journalism here

The Anointed Son

that will be long remembered and sets an important precedent. Make no mistake: This decision creates a chilling effect all right, but not what Bailey had hoped it would do to Gentry.

The decision, written by Justice Michael Douglas, should freeze any attempts by lawyers to try to go around the shield law by making frivolous accusations about a journalist without a scintilla of evidence, using the courts to deter aggressive investigative reporting. It is monumentally important.

First, the court dismissed Bailey's contention that a journalist needs an affidavit to prove the shield law applies. That is a patently ridiculous burden of proof, which the court shredded.

Second, and more important, the court exposed what Guinn and Bailey were doing and declared it unacceptable. This is the critical part of the decision:

<u>*The statute broadly protects any information that is gathered in the course of preparing a news story, as well as the sources of such information. While Aspen (Guinn's company) asserts that it has only sought information relating to Gentry in her personal capacity, the record demonstrates that this is not accurate. In particular, Aspen's claims in the action below allege that the investors improperly influenced Gentry to produce news stories favorable to them and unfavorable to Aspen. Thus, it appears from the face of the subpoena that, when read in the context of Aspen's claims, Aspen has requested the information sought in order to affirm its suspicions about Gentry's motivation for producing those news stories. Indeed, Aspen's arguments in the opposition to the motion to quash and in its writ petition confirm that this is its reason for serving Gentry with the subpoena. In other words, although Aspen claims that it is not seeking Gentry's sources because it already knows whom those sources are, the circumstances of this case demonstrate that Aspen actually is effectively seeking to confirm the identities of Gentry's sources. As the identity of a reporter's source is information that is protected under the plain language of the news shield statute, see NRS 49.275 (protecting from disclosure "the source of any information procured or obtained*</u>

by" a reporter), we conclude that the information sought was facially protected under the news shield statute.

I have only one word: Bravo.

There was a footnote, too, that is crucial here: *To the extent that this is not Aspen's purpose, Aspen has not explained how the information sought might be relevant or lead to relevant information regarding its claims or defenses in the action below.*

Exactly. No evidence. Not a whit.

And so we have a decision that likely will gain resonance in national media law circles as Nevada's shield law, already potent, grows more so. This would not have happened without the tremendous talents of Don Campbell, my lawyer for two and a half decades who immediately saw the importance of Gentry's case and took it on with his usual fervor. His briefs were brilliant, his argument before the justices earlier this year compelling.

Campbell had help, too, from his associates at his law firm, including Colby Williams and Hunter Campbell, and from two other attorneys who deserve kudos: Mark Hinueber, who despite being the counsel for a rival news organization was as supportive as anyone in this matter and rallied people to the cause; and Maggie McLetchie, the former ACLU attorney and one of the best in the state who leant her talents to the case.

All of Nevada's journalists now and in the future are in their debt.

I am thrilled for my friend and colleague that those who manipulated the legal process to try to destroy her reputation have instead been exposed for what I always said they were: Leeches sucking a vindictive client for all they could in pursuit of a case no lawyer with any character would have taken on.

The Anointed Son

And I am heartened that I live in a state that, for all of its problems, has a journalistic community that comes together for one of its own, a group of lawyers who are willing to sacrifice for what they believe is an important cause and a high court that should make everyone proud.

I thank you. Excuse me: We thank you.

Sadly, that whole "we" thing wouldn't last much longer.

77: ON THE HOOK

By the time a federal judge confirmed the FDIC's $22.5 million judgment against Guinn and company, Jeff and Monica Guinn had filed bankruptcy, and Kenny Guinn, who had guaranteed the $4.7 million loan secured by Aspen's office building, was dead.

But Kenny and Dema Guinn's Irrevocable Asset Management Trust, which also guaranteed one of the Community Bank Loans, somehow escaped paying the piper.

Developer Kent Barry has made and lost fortunes in his lifetime. It was little wonder when Barry, having been on the hook for tens of millions of dollars in unpaid loans from his projects with Jeff Guinn, momentarily appeared to escape relatively unscathed from Aspen's Waterloo. Same story for Aspen's one-time vice-president and Jeff Guinn's development partner, Sean Corrigan.

Here's what Barry told the Ruthes' attorney Dennis Prince under oath in March of 2013:

Q: Are you a guarantor on any loan that was made or arranged by or through Aspen Financial Services?
A: At this time?
Q: At this time?
A: Yes.
Q: Which loans?
A: Coronado Eastern, slash, Retail. And Escalade Venture, LLC, and that's it.
Q: Okay. What about Coronado Horizon Boulder?
A: That's been closed out.
Q: What do you mean it's. been closed out?
A: It was sold.

The Anointed Son

Q: And were you released of your guaranty?
A: We were.
Q: Okay. How did that work?
A: Found a buyer. Actually, we found two or three. All of the offers went out for a vote to investors. Once the threshold of 51 percent was reached, it was deemed approved and sold. All funds were distributed, then, back to the investors.
Q: Okay. Who else was released of their guaranty other than you? Mr. Guinn?
A: On which loan?
Q: The Coronado Horizon Boulder loan.
A: Yes. Mr. Guinn.
Q: And when did that property sell?
A: Approximately May of 2012.
Q: And what was the deficiency between the amount that was owed under the loan by Coronado Horizon Boulder to the investors and how much that was received? What was the difference?
A: I'm not sure.
Q: Approximately.
A: 15 million.
Q: Okay. So you were forgiven $15 million of indebtedness; is that correct?
MR. LIEBMAN: Objection. Calls for a legal conclusion. You can answer.
Q: (BY MR. PRINCE) Is that correct?
A: Please ask the question again.
Q: Right. I mean you were forgiven $15 million of indebtedness; correct?
MR. LIEBMAN: Same objection. You can respond.
THE WITNESS: I believe so, yes.
...
Q: Okay. We just looked at your financial statement. You seemed to have a net worth of almost $20 million of your own. I mean did you make any contribution toward interest payments by that point?
A: No, I had not.

Q: What was Mr. Guinn's net worth around that time as your co-borrower and guarantor?
A: I have no idea.
Q: You never discussed that?
A: I've never seen his financial statement ever.
Q: Well, you made application to your co-guarantors on certain loans.
A: Yes.
Q: But you're unaware of what his financial status was?
A: I have no idea what it was.
Q: You never inquired what it was even though he's a co-guarantor on a loan?
A: No, I didn't.
Q: Why wouldn't you?
MR. LIEBMAN: Why would he?
THE WITNESS: I just never did.
Q: (BY MR. PRINCE) Well, I'm not on the hook for $50 million of loans. I mean wouldn't you be worried about whether your co-borrower could pay back $50 million in loans?
A: No, I wasn't worried about it.
Q: Well, why weren't you worried about it? Because it was through Aspen?
A: No. Because it was Jeff Guinn. And —
Q: What does that mean?
A: Well, it means I knew his financial status was...
Q: Was unlimited?
A: Was not unlimited, but it was as good or better than mine.
Q: Do you think it was better than yours?
A: Yes.
Q: By how much?
A: I have no idea. I've never seen his financial statement.[115]

Guinn's development partner Sean Corrigan testified in the Ruthe case

---

[115] Sean Corrigan deposition June 5, 2013

that he personally lost more than $2.5 million on Aspen loans gone bad.[116]

Corrigan noted he had a $2.25 million judgment from City National Bank for an unsecured line of credit.

Corrigan also discussed the Community Bank loans taken over by the FDIC.

"I have a unsecured line of credit judgment against me from the FDIC. And I think that amount is the approximate neighborhood of $700,000, Dennis."[117]

Barry and Corrigan grossly underestimated their liability back in 2013.

On July 7, 2015, with Jeff and Monica in bankruptcy and Kenny's obligation somehow wiped out by a bankruptcy judge, Corrigan and Barry were left holding the bag on a $22.5 million judgment for the now-defunct Community Bank loans in favor of the FDIC.

---

[116] Sean Corrigan deposition June 5, 2013 p.9

[117] Sean Corrigan deposition June 5, 2013

78: FRIDAY THE 13TH

I'm not superstitious, but perhaps it's worth noting the date — Friday, March 13, 2015 — when I ran into Dema Guinn at Channel 10.

KSNV owner Jim Rogers died in 2014. In November, Sinclair Broadcasting purchased the station and quickly moved to cancel Ralston Reports and fire Jon. I was to stay to do investigative reporting and produce and anchor my business program, Vegas Inc.

Meanwhile, Jon was working to get our program a new home. In February of 2015, I left KSNV to join Jon at Vegas PBS.

The newest iteration of our program had been on the air at PBS for two weeks when I ran into Dema Guinn.

I returned from lunch to find the Vegas PBS general manager, Tom Axtell, talking with Mary Dean Martin, a public relations maven I've known for decades. I hadn't even taken notice of the woman standing with Martin. I looked up into the cold gaze of Dema Guinn, who looked incredibly good for a woman her age.

I stuck out my hand. "Hi, Mrs. Guinn. Nice to see you."

She screwed up what had been such a pretty face a second earlier and barely choked out a "hello." After a few awkward seconds, I excused myself and went to my office.

That evening, in the control room after the program, Tom Axtell asked me why I ventured over to say hello. I noted that I'd only noticed Mary Dean Martin at first, plus I added, I had no reason to avoid Mrs. Guinn.

As I had been taught long ago by Ned Day, don't report anything about anyone that prevents you from looking that person in the eye. I had no

The Anointed Son

problem looking Dema Guinn in the eye.

"Why? Did she tell you to fire me?" I asked Axtell, remembering her earlier efforts to have my job.

"No, she didn't say that," Axtell replied. "She just said you're dishonest. And she's joining our board."

Without skipping a beat, Jon chimed in, "It's been nice working with you."

Dishonest! I couldn't imagine a more general indictment of an employee—a new one at that! Tom Axtell didn't know me at all. I immediately sensed a change in his attitude toward me that would permeate what was left of our brief working relationship.

That night, I also heard Axtell tell another employee that he was hoping to pack the KLVX board with politically powerful people who "could not be denied by the policy makers" undertaking the latest attempt to deconsolidate the Clark County School District—a move Axtell feared would threaten Channel 10's school district funding.

A week later, on March 20, Axtell called me into his office to tell me he had a report that I'd been overheard saying "bullshit." I apologized and told him it wouldn't happen again. Then he said he'd had a report that "surprised" him: that I was abusive to our producer, Priya Mathew.

I was in shock. With no help from the Vegas PBS crew, which seemed overwhelmed by the production, Priya was the only reason we were getting the program on the air. I would have kissed her feet at the time.

"Did you ask Priya?" I inquired, shocked by the allegation and certain Priya would be able to put Axtell's concerns to rest.

"I'm not going to open that door," he replied.

Now I was stunned. A manager was accusing me of being abusive to a co-worker, yet refusing to investigate?

I went home and wrote Axtell an email saying I thought it was unfair to leave the allegation hanging without any investigation. No reply.

Could his rapid change in attitude toward me have anything to do with Dema Guinn? I doubted she was directly responsible, but couldn't help but wonder if her warning that I was "dishonest" had poisoned the well with my new employer.

The next month was a nightmare. Jon was demanding we add new elements even as the general manager at Reno PBS was demanding "consistently flawless" production of our live TV show (an oxymoron) before adding any bells and whistles. What's more, the station managers were blaming Priya and me for not getting the show posted on the web rapidly, even though their stations lacked the technological ability at that point for a rapid turnaround.

Jon told me he had complained to school district officials and others who he hoped would put heat on the general managers. The general managers, who lacked a basic understanding of the limitations of their own equipment, in turn, put heat on us to perform impossible tasks.

The 2015 legislative session was tailor-made for TV. The state's Republican governor was proposing a tax increase. The usual suspects on the right, mostly rural fundamentalists, were working overtime to impose their antiquated agenda on the state's population centers, including a controversial effort to determine which restrooms transgender students could access in public school bathrooms. And the anti-union fervor that gripped other parts of the nation had taken hold in Carson City.

Our program, known in its previous iterations as the place for political news, was limited to one, maybe two topics a day, thanks to the edict not to add elements until we'd achieved flawless production.

Feeling as if we were reporting in a vacuum, I emailed our crew and

The Anointed Son

management in mid-April after a phone call with Jon that we hoped to add a headline segment the following week.

Crickets.

The next week, I sent out another email restating our intention and asking for feedback. The gentleman listed on my job description as my supervisor, Brent Boynton, responded, requesting that I touch bases with the director, who had been off work the previous week.

On Tuesday, we initiated a headline segment. The next night, we followed up with another headline segment. My phone rang right after the program.

"Dana. This is Kurt Mische. I'm on speaker in my office with Jon Ralston. WHO THE HELL AUTHORIZED A HEADLINE SEGMENT? AND SINCE WHEN DO WE DO COMMENTARY?" screamed the voice at the other end of the phone.

Since when don't we do commentary? My mind shot to the news release from the PBS stations announcing Ralston Live: "*Ralston will bring his own brand of news, commentary and analysis to PBS.*"

At the same time, Jon and I both began to explain that I had informed the crew of our plans via email.

"I DON'T READ YOUR EMAIL," the voice screamed again. "YOU SEND TOO MANY GODDAMN EMAILS."

I wanted to cry. I had been begging for better communication (via email), only to be told they weren't even being read. Future efforts to turn out a quality production suddenly seemed futile.

I'd never met Mische, but had heard from Jon and others about his profanity-laced tirades directed at the crew after programs originating in Reno.

When I had asked about Mische's TV experience, Jon told me that a producer in Reno had said "Jon, Kurt doesn't know anything about television."

I tried to get a sentence in between Mische's outbursts.

"I told Jon the other day that maybe I should look for something else," I managed at barely a whisper.

"SEE, JON! THESE ARE THE THINGS SHE'S SAYING IN THE HALLS OF CHANNEL TEN! SHE'S TURNING YOUR CREW AGAINST YOU!" the voice exploded again.

I wanted to laugh. But instead, I cried. And hung up. I walked to my computer and quickly typed up my resignation from the program I'd produced for fourteen years.

Jon called thirty minutes later.

"Well," he said. "I haven't been reamed like that in years, Dana." He said he'd just left Mische's office and that he'd worked everything out.

"It's too late," I told him. "I emailed my resignation."

"C'mon. I hope this is just a typical Dana Gentry resignation."

Then, without skipping a beat, Jon added, "Do you want me to help you find a job?"

I was crying hysterically. "No," I choked out.

I was shocked. I attempted to rescind my resignation the next day on the advice of an attorney, but was unceremoniously relieved of my duties, with Vegas PBS manager Tom Axtell telling me that his staffers found me to be mean and intimidating—because I'm tall.

The Anointed Son

The realization of what was happening began to hit me a few days later. I asked Jon in an email if anyone else had witnessed Mische screaming on the phone. Jon told me to stop contacting him if I was trying to get information.

I was crushed. What on earth had happened? I had to know.

It occurred to me that given Vegas PBS's school district affiliation, its communications were public record. I filed a public records request with the Clark County School District for any correspondence to or from Tom Axtell that mentioned my name.

It took months for the school district to comply with the request, but it was worth the wait.

The "smoking gun" was an email from Ralston to the two PBS general managers, encouraging them to quickly accept my resignation, and written by Jon about five minutes after he told me he hoped I wasn't really quitting.

Jon's duplicity was stunning. Our collaboration and friendship ended without as much as a mention in his daily email newsletter. Ralston, who pontificated on just about everything, was apparently at a loss for words.

PBS cancelled Ralston Live a year after I left. Sadly, I felt some smug consolation knowing the program I produced for fourteen years lasted only a year without me.

Did Dema Guinn poison the well at PBS, sealing my fate just two weeks into my new job by branding me "dishonest?"

Regardless of whether she succeeded, I'm relatively certain that was her intent.

79: NO HELP FROM DAD

Despite voluminous public records detailing Kenny and Dema Guinn's investments in their son Jeff's hard money brokerage, in deposition, Jeff Guinn denied receiving help from his father, preferring instead to portray himself, like his father, as a self-made man.

Attorney Dennis Prince: Did you, obviously, your father knew many people in the business community in Las Vegas. Correct?
Jeff Guinn: I'm sure he did.
Q: Well, did you use those contacts?
A: No. My father wouldn't help me.
Q: What's that?
A: My father wouldn't help me.
Q: He never helped you?
A: No.
Q: Never?
A: To get business?
Q: Yes.
A: Never.
Q: Never once?
A: Never once.
Q: Not even at Aspen, never helped you get business?
A: Never.
Q: Not one single time?
A: No.[118]

The truth was that Jeff Guinn used the First Couple's fortune like a piggy bank to make loans to the very people who helped put Kenny

---

[118] Jeff Guinn p. 82-83

The Anointed Son

Guinn in office—his campaign contributors.

Kenny Guinn designated his sons, Jeff and Steve, as co-trustees of the First Couple's blind trust, a practice that's prohibited in most states that regulate blind trusts held by public officials.[119] Nevada law makes

---

[119] In California and Florida, for instance, the trustee may not be a family member, business associate or official appointed by the grantor. In New Jersey the trust may not contain assets that must be recorded (i.e., real estate) nor be invested in an industry regulated by the official.

-Florida law prohibits child of public official from acting as trustee.

(a) The appointed trustee must be a bank, trust company, or other institutional fiduciary or an individual who is an attorney, certified public accountant, broker, or investment advisor. If the trustee is an individual or if the trustee is a bank, trust company, or other institutional fiduciary, the individual responsible for managing the trust may not be:

    1. **The public officer's spouse, child, parent, grandparent, grandchild, brother, sister, parent-in-law, brother-in-law, sister-in-law, aunt, uncle, or first cousin, or the spouse of any such person;**

    2. A person who is an elected or appointed public officer or a public employee;

    3. A person who has been appointed to serve in an agency by the public officer or by a public officer or public employee supervised by the public officer; or

    4. A business associate or principal of the public officer.)

(New Jersey: 1. For those situations where a blind trust may be utilized by a State officer or employee or special State officer or employee, his/her spouse or domestic partner or dependent children, and approved by the Commission, such trust shall contain the following characteristics:
a. The trust shall not contain investments or assets in which the holder's ownership right or interest is required to be recorded in a public office or those assets whose permanency makes transfer by the trustee improbable or impractical; these investments or assets would include, but not be limited to,

no mention of blind trusts.

Kenny Guinn's initial financial disclosure, filed during his 1998 candidacy for governor, includes Aspen Financial as a source of income.

What was the extent of Kenny Guinn's involvement in Aspen Financial, his son's brokerage?

I wondered whether Governor Guinn may have had an ownership interest in his son's company or whether the reference in his financial disclosure pertained to interest earned on investments.

I reconstructed the First Couple's investments through the Guinn

---

businesses, real estate, security interests in personal property and mortgages;
b. The trust shall contain a clear statement of its purpose, namely, to remove from the grantor control and knowledge of investment of trust assets so that conflicts between grantor's responsibilities and duties as a public employee or public officer and his or her private business or financial interests will be eliminated;
c. The trust shall be irrevocable, and shall be terminated only upon the death of the public employee or public officer or upon termination of his or her status as a public employee or public officer whichever shall first occur;
d. The trustee shall be directed not to disclose to the grantor any information about any of the assets in the trust;
...

g. A provision shall be included in the trust agreement prohibiting the trustee from investing the trust property in corporations or businesses which do a significant amount of business with the State of New Jersey or from knowingly making any investment in a corporation, business or venture over which the grantor has regulatory or supervisory authority by virtue of his or her official position;
h. The grantor shall retain no control over the trustee nor shall he or she be permitted to make any recommendations or suggestions as to the trust property;
-August 29, 2006 New Jersey

The Anointed Son

Irrevocable Asset Management Trust, the blind trust.

What I found was mind-blowing.

With Kenny Guinn's public integrity shielded by a "blind trust," Jeff Guinn used his parents' money to fund almost 300 loans between 1999, Guinn's first year in office, and 2006, when his term ended. The borrowers in eighty percent of those loans were contributors (or corporate alter egos) to Kenny Guinn's gubernatorial campaign.

The face amount of the Guinn blind trust's loans to Aspen borrowers totaled a staggering $36 million, which earned Kenny and Dema Guinn between 12 and 15 percent interest.

Contrary to Jeff Guinn's testimony that his father never helped him, thanks in large part to the Guinn blind trust, Aspen Financial graduated from brokering modest loans in the $1 million range to syndicating $25 million deals.

From November of 1997 through November 1998, the year preceding Kenny Guinn's election as governor, Kenny and Dema's Guinn Family Trust funded 20 loans. All but five were to campaign contributors — among them, developers Barry Becker, Jim Zeiter, Jordan Primack, and E.A. Collins.

On October 10, 1997, Aspen Financial brokered a $6.4 million loan to Russell Dorn and Roland Sturm, partners in Developers of Nevada. Kenny and Dema Guinn funded $543,000 of that loan.

On November 3, 1997, Aspen Financial funded a $2.1 million loan to a joint venture between the Developers of Nevada and Olympic Land, LLC, owned by Southern Highlands developer Garry Goett.

Kenny and Dema Guinn's Family Trust contributed $669,200, a third of the loan.

Nine days later, Developers of Nevada contributed $10,000 to Guinn's campaign.

Goett's Olympic Land, LLC contributed $2500 to the Guinn campaign on November 17, 1997.

Two months later, on January 16, 1998, Kenny and Dema's trust funded $115,000 of a $240,000 loan brokered by Aspen Financial to the Developers of Nevada.

On February 10, 1998, Kenny and Dema's trust funded $100,000 of a $346,500 loan arranged by Aspen Financial for the Developers of Nevada.

A few weeks later, on February 27, the Guinns funded $173,332, a third of an Aspen-brokered loan of $518,000, to the Developers of Nevada.

On his financial disclosure filed June 2, 1998, Kenny Guinn noted the Developers of Nevada as a source of income, but failed to disclose the interest he held in the variety of real estate parcels securing those and other loans, as required by law.

On November 5, 1997, Kenny and Dema Guinn's trust funded just under $45,000 of a $567,500 loan brokered by Aspen Financial to Pageantry Homes. Nine days later, Pageantry Communities contributed $5000 to Kenny Guinn's campaign.

In November of 1997, Distinctive Homes contributed $1000 to Guinn's campaign. The following month, Kenny and Dema Guinn funded $96,500 of a $610,000 loan to Distinctive Homes brokered by Aspen Financial.

Primack Homes, operated by developer Jordan Primack, contributed $1000 to Guinn's campaign on November 7, 1997. A month later, Kenny and Dema Guinn funded $144,199 of an Aspen Financial brokered loan of $730,000 to Primack Homes. Primack Realty contributed $500 to the governor's campaign in February 1998. Aspen, with help from the governor's blind trust, would fund two more loans to Primack that year.

The Anointed Son

In August of 1998, Aspen Financial funded a $300,000 loan to Las Palmas, a development owned by Barry Becker and Jim Zeiter.

Becker Investment contributed $2000 to Guinn campaign just days before the election, on October 31, 1998.

In the Spring of 1999, the new governor formed the Guinn Irrevocable Asset Management Trust, the "blind trust," which funded $4.3 million in 33 loans that year. The borrowers on twenty-seven of the loans were campaign contributors, including Christopher Stuhmer of Christopher Homes, Don White of Pageantry Homes, and developers Barry Becker, Richard Plaster, Ken Gragson, and Howard Bulloch, the force behind the failed SkyVue observation wheel at the south end of the Las Vegas Strip.

In 2000, Jeff Guinn invested a cumulative $7 million dollars from his parents' blind trust in 57 loans brokered by Aspen Financial. 44 of the 57 borrowers were contributors to Kenny Guinn's 1998 campaign. Among them were attorney Al Flangas and developers E.A. Collins, Jim Zeiter, Richard Plaster, and Susan Mardian. Also among the borrowers relying on Governor and Mrs. Guinn's money that year was their own son, Jeff, who used about $1 million to fund several loans to companies he owned.

The governor's blind trust funded forty-five loans in 2001. Thirty-three were to campaign contributors. One of the twelve loans not made to campaign contributors was granted to the governor's own Lt. Governor Lorraine Hunt.

On March 29, 2001 Lt. Gov. Hunt filed the state's required financial disclosure form and listed no debts. Less than two months later, Hunt borrowed $1.1 million from Aspen Financial. Governor Guinn's trust invested $47,876.

I asked Hunt if she had any qualms as Lt. Governor about borrowing from the Governor.

"We were all in banking. I wouldn't have thought about it," she said during a phone interview.

The governor's blind trust funded $1.8 million in loan proceeds in 2002. Twenty-eight of the thirty-three borrowers that year were contributors to Kenny Guinn's 1998 campaign.

The blind trust's investments soared to $5.1 million in 2003. Forty-three of the forty-eight borrowers were contributors to the governor's campaign.

2004 saw the governor's blind trust fund $4.3 million via forty-eight loans. Thirty-eight of the borrowers were Guinn contributors.

2005 was the height of the real estate boom in Southern Nevada. The Guinn Irrevocable Asset Management Trust invested $8.3 million in twelve loans brokered by Aspen that year (eight of the twelve borrowers were Guinn contributors) as the hard money lender set a record pace—closing multiple transactions a month—except for June, when public records reveal the Guinn blind trust was inactive.

That was the month Jeff Guinn went to rehab under an assumed name.

In 2006, the governor's blind trust funded eleven loans—nine of them to Guinn former campaign contributors. Among them: uber-developer John Ritter.

$36 million. 304 loans. 80 percent to campaign contributors.

All of it concealed in a blind trust.

Even if Nevada law specifically sanctioned installing your children as trustees of a "blind trust," wouldn't Governor Guinn have realized the folly of claiming ignorance of investments directed by his sons?

Why, I wondered, would Kenny Guinn abuse the spirit, if not the letter, of the financial disclosure law?

Several possibilities came to mind.

Was Governor Guinn reluctant to publicly associate himself with an industry fraught with controversy and high-profile failures, an industry

The Anointed Son

regulated by the state?

And there was the prospect of how to disclose an interest in so many properties without drawing scrutiny. In some instances, the Guinn Trust bought in and out of a loan in a matter of days or even hours.

On September 13, 1999, the governor's blind trust invested a relatively small amount, $11,655 in a loan to New Homes, a company owned by Richard Plaster. The Guinn Irrevocable Asset Management Trust appeared on the list of investors distributed to all who had a share at close of escrow. Two days later, on September 15, the governor's blind trust sold almost all of its interest in the loan.

On July 13, 2001, the Guinn Irrevocable Asset Management Trust funded 100% of a $77,000 loan to Blue Valley LLC. The same day, the Trust assigned, or sold, 80% of its interest to other lender/investors. Former Clark County Commissioner Jay Bingham is a principal in Blue Valley LLC.

Is there a logical explanation for the erratic trading?

Did Governor Guinn hide his investments for nefarious reasons?

Was there a quid pro quo?

Did Guinn, who as governor was privy to the kind of inside information that is invaluable to developers, help Aspen borrowers get a jump on the competition?

Did the borrowers choose Aspen Financial because it offered the best loan terms, or because they wanted to curry favor with the governor?

The purpose of ethics laws is to avoid even the perception of a conflict.

The Guinns' blind trust noted it was created *"...to avoid the appearance of a conflict of interest by Kenny Guinn in executing the Office of Governor of the State of Nevada."*

Does a blind trust satisfy Nevada's financial disclosure law?

United States Senator Dean Heller was Nevada's Secretary of State during Guinn's first term. Heller has repeatedly declined to answer any questions for this book, including whether he believes a blind trust satisfies the requirements of Nevada's financial disclosure form.

Former state and local lawmaker and 2018 candidate for State Treasurer, Bob Beers, says beneficial interest must be disclosed, regardless of whether it's held in trust, blind or not.

Nevada State Senator and candidate for Clark County Commission Tick Segerblom says he doesn't think the state can legislate blind trusts.

"The press and political parties need to call out anyone who tries to claim a blind trust when the trustee is a relative — that's not a blind trust."

Segerblom said politicians who employ a blind trust should be questioned about the structure, "what kind of transactions it will engage in, and who will make those decisions."

"I am concerned that the trust was used to make loans to contributors." Segerblom went on to say close proximity between the loans and contributions could be even more problematic

Current Secretary of State Barbara Cegavske says a blind trust meets the requirements of the disclosure form, as does former Secretary of State Ross Miller's election guru, Matt Griffin.

Nevada Lt. Governor Mark Hutchison, a trust attorney, former ethics commissioner and lawmaker, declined to offer an opinion on blind trusts or relatives as trustees, and told me he has no interest in helping me write a book about Kenny Guinn.

Guinn is not the only governor to have taken cover behind a blind trust. Legal challenges to Florida Governor Rick Scott's attempts to shield his wealth via a blind trust have failed, and the controversy remains a

The Anointed Son

topic of public debate.

In some other states, where public officials are prohibited from investing in industries regulated by the state and from having relatives administer blind trusts, Governor Guinn would have been disqualified on both counts. But not in corporate-friendly Nevada, which simply lacks regulation, rendering blind trusts better suited for hiding assets than avoiding conflicts.

Guinn was a political neophyte, but even he had to know that earning 15 percent interest on millions of dollars invested with his son's company would raise questions about his adherence to the strict state regulation the scandal-plagued hard money lending industry required.

If Kenny Guinn had been serious about blinding his assets while in office, it seems unlikely he would have named his sons as trustees.

And with his sons serving as co-trustees, was the Governor truly blind to his investments?

It would take years to learn the truth, which would be stranger than fiction, and would come from none other than Jeff Guinn's brother, Steve.

80: Blind No More

Despite extensive inquiries, no one in the Guinn camp had any interest in answering my questions about the extent of Governor Guinn's detachment from his investments.

I resigned myself to putting the matter to rest in that dreaded, dark closet every journalist keeps—the place where unanswered questions go.

In 2016, with just months until Jeff Guinn went on trial for bankruptcy fraud, his brother Steve sat for a deposition in the Ruthe case.

It was Jeff's brother, the governor's other son, who would flip on the light switch in the Closet of Unanswered Questions, confirming what I already suspected and forever altering my perception of Kenny Guinn.

Las Vegas, despite its growth, remains a very small town.

Jeff Guinn's brother Steve and Donna Ruthe's attorney, Dennis Prince, are childhood acquaintances.

Perhaps Steve Guinn felt comfortable when Prince eased into questioning his old friend under oath in June of 2016. The line of questioning Kenny Guinn's blind trust, the Guinn Irrevocable Asset Management Trust.

Q: Dennis Prince: What was the purpose of the Asset Management Trust?
A: It was set up in 1999 when my dad went into office. And he spent a lot of time up in Carson City, obviously. So when these loans went though, it was really set up for me to be able to sign and kind of process these loans through the system, and it was his investment trust that he put through Mon—put through Aspen. ...

Q: Okay. Have you ever heard or did you ever hear your dad refer to the Asset Management trust as a blind trust?
A: No.[120]

NO? Could it be the governor never admonished his sons not to talk to him about the blind trust's investments at Aspen? They signed the document. Did they not read it?

Q: Okay. And as a trustee of – how long were you the trustee of the Irrevocable Asset Management Trust?
A: I believe it was from 1999 until when he got out of office in 2007. ...
Q: Okay. What did you–what were your powers as a trustee of the Asset Management trust?
A: I essentially just sign loan documents, review them.
Q: What loan documents?
A: Loans that the Guinn Irrevocable Asset Management Trust was investing in Aspen Financial Services.
Q: Okay. Were you involved in managing any other assets other than loans through Aspen Financial?
A: No.
Q: Okay. Were those the only investments, to your knowledge, that the Guinn Irrevocable Asset Management Trust invested in during that eight-year period?
A: To my knowledge, yes.
...
Q: Okay. When your father went into office and you became a trustee of the Irrevocable Asset Management Trust, what investment authority did you have?
A: I really didn't have any investment authority. When the documents came to me, my brother and dad had already spoken, and I was essentially kind of reviewing them and signing them and getting ready for closing.

What?? "...my brother and dad had already spoken..."

Maybe Steve Guinn had misspoken. I read on.

A: Okay. So – okay. So for that eight-year period between 1999 and

---

[120]Steve Guinn deposition p. 15

2007...
Q: Mm-hmm.

Even the unflappable Dennis Prince appeared to be at a loss for words. Steve Guinn, perhaps unwittingly, was shining a bright light into what was clearly a not-so-blind trust.

Q: Okay. Now, where did the statements for the Guinn Irrevocable Asset Management Trust go? Where were they sent to monthly?
A: They were sent to Aspen.
Q: Say that again?
A: They were sent to Aspen. Either Aspen Financial or to my dad, either one. But they were kept at Aspen. I know that.
Q: Okay.
A: My dad had a file there.
Q: Okay. So your—so the—explain what you mean by that statement, your dad had a file there. What do you mean?
A: That's where the documents were kept.
Q: Okay.[121] ...
A: My dad had a file cabinet over there that he kept so when he was in town, in Las Vegas, he'd come in, and that's where he'd kind of review his files and stuff.
Q: Okay.
A: It was my understanding that Jeff and him were under conversation, and that's the way it always worked. When I talked with my dad, he said the same thing.
And—
Q: Okay.
A: It was—I was really nothing more than a facilitator signing the documents, the closing papers, to get it closed.[122]
...
A: My dad told me kind of what it was set up for to begin with, and it was just a way to facilitate the loans and get them closed and moving on. ...
Q: What did he specifically tell you why it was formed?
A: He—he told me that being up in Mon—being up in Carson City, it allowed us to—the money was going back and forth so quick on those

---

[121] Steve Guinn p. 18-19

[122] Steve Guinn P. 19

loans, as everybody was doing at Aspen. He said "It's just a more convenient way. If you can put yourself on this, we can have you sign, and you can help close the loans while I'm up in Carson City."
Q: Okay.
A: The other thing he said, too, is he just didn't want to—for whatever reason, he says, "It's just better off that, you know, Jeff and I talk over phone, deal with these things, and we can discuss them, and it's more effective time."[123]

…

Q: And did he tell you what his investment goals were at Aspen through the Asset Management Trust?
A: My father?
Q: Yeah.
A: No. Every once in a while, he would discuss what he had invested over there with me, but that was about it.[124]

Without realizing it, (or did he?) the governor's son was rapidly eroding the opacity of his father's blind trust.

Kenny Guinn, according to his son, was acutely aware of how his money was being invested. His financial disclosure filed with the state was at odds with his son's testimony and apparently designed to conceal his investments rather than shield the governor from conflicts of interest.

According to his son's testimony, Guinn, one of the most beloved governors in state history, deceived the people of Nevada for eight years. In doing so the governor reaped millions in profits from deals with prominent developers and campaign contributors, and avoided scrutiny from media, regulators, and voters.

My book—this book, neatly tied up and undergoing fact-checking, was suddenly and glaringly incomplete.

Another rewrite was in order.

---

[123] Steve Guinn p. 25
[124] Steve Guinn p. 26

81: Expert Witness

Jeff Guinn's attorneys hired David Goldwater as an expert witness in their client's bankruptcy fraud trial. Guinn and Goldwater had been on opposite sides in 1999 when Goldwater, then a Nevada assemblyman, tried to shore up Nevada mortgage lending law. At issue that year was the state's disclosure form, which the law required be signed before brokers accepted any investor money. It was a key reform aimed at avoiding a repeat of high-profile hard money meltdowns.

Here's what Goldwater, the former lawmaker turned expert witness, wrote in the Executive Summary of his report in defense of Jeff Guinn:

"The regulatory structure of (Nevada Revised Statute) 645B provided protection for lenders/investors and mortgage brokers by requiring certain disclosures. The severe economic recession exposed the risk in ALL lending. While it was unfortunate investors/lenders lost money, these were very risky investment/loans. **If the required information was disclosed to the Plaintiffs**, (emphasis added) it was not the fault of the mortgage broker when the investment/loans were not successful."

Goldwater repeated the same caveat dozens of times throughout his expert report.

Didn't Goldwater know that Guinn had already claimed the disclosure law was too onerous, and that he had a pass from the state to ignore it?

The state-mandated disclosures were executed after the close of escrow, and in violation of the law, in all but a handful of the twenty-seven loans at issue in the Ruthe litigation.

Goldwater also noted that hard money loans were of a short duration and not a permanent source of financing. He's right. But Aspen Financial's business model depended on serial refinancing, sometimes of the same loan for a span of five or six years and, remarkably, sometimes with few improvements made to the property.

82: The Governor's Grandson

It's one thing to be sued by investors. And it's a bigger thing to be investigated by the FBI. But being accused by your own child of chronic sexual and physical abuse is an entirely different realm. That's the position in which Jeff Guinn found himself in late September 2016, on the eve of his trial on charges of bankruptcy fraud.

Colton Guinn professed not to know of his father's impending trial when he called me two days before the opening statements. Was it a set-up? Was Jeff Guinn using his own child to somehow manipulate the proceedings in the final hours before the long-awaited and often-postponed trial? Was he looking for grounds to declare a mistrial? My mind whirled through countless possibilities as Colton Guinn recounted his story, which to this day, remains both unfathomable and deeply troubling.

What Colton Guinn told me could do his father no good under any circumstances. That didn't make it true, just unlikely to be a set-up.

But did I want to report it? Given the highly sensitive nature, I would have to take even more care than usual.

And would the police even investigate the young man's claims, given Metro's cozy history with Jeff Guinn?

My first call was to Metro Detective Michael Fortunato, who Colton, a young adult at the time, said was investigating his allegations. I mentioned Jeff Guinn's history of co-opting cops and wondered if Metro would really look into Colton's claims. Detective Fortunato assured me he was "actively investigating" Colton's allegations. He also confirmed he'd talked with Dema Guinn.

Jeff Guinn did not respond to my email regarding his son's allegations.

The Anointed Son

Monica Guinn hung up on me when I called her cell.

I had enough to go on, but I wanted more. I put in a call to the one other person Colton claimed was aware of the abuse: his grandmother, former First Lady Dema Guinn.

No answer. I didn't leave a message. I wanted to call back, and didn't want to put Mrs. Guinn on guard. But I didn't need to worry about that. Less than an hour later, my phone rang.

"Hello," I answered.

"Hello, this is Dema. I got a call from this number."

"Hi, Mrs. Guinn, it's Dana Gentry. I hope you're well." I fully expected a click. But it didn't come.

"Hello, Dana."

"Mrs. Guinn," I started hurriedly, afraid she'd hang up at any moment. "I spoke recently with your grandson, Colton. And with a police detective who says he's talked with you about Colton's allegations against Jeff and Monica."

"Yes, I spoke with him. Dana, Colton is our problem child. He's out for money. He wants to live the lifestyle he used to have with his mom and dad. He feels that's been taken from him. This is nothing more than a shakedown."

Colton, she said, claimed to be owed millions of dollars.

I was floored that she was talking with me. And she was so forthcoming. Maybe she was right. Still, erroneous claims of sexual abuse at the hands of a parent are rare.

"Colton wasn't raised right. He was rewarded for bad behavior. It wasn't the way Kenny and I wanted him to be raised," she added.

Did she realize she was casting aspersions on her own son's parenting?

The conversation was surreal.

Mrs. Guinn remarked she hadn't seen me on TV and asked what I was doing.

I told her I'd quit my job at Channel 10 shortly after she told Tom Axtell I was dishonest, which she quickly denied.

"I don't know why he'd say such a thing," she protested.

I told her I'd been writing a book about her husband and Jeff. I asked if she knew anything about the blind trust. She said she didn't.

I asked if she knew if the governor was aware of the investments he was making while in office. Mrs. Guinn responded that of course he knew. They had all their money invested in Aspen.

I noted that the Guinn Irrevocable Trust was designed to blind the governor to his investments. She responded that maybe Kenny just knew his money was in Aspen, but not the specific loans. When I told her that her own son, Steve, testified that his father was aware of the individual investments, Mrs. Guinn pleaded with me to stop "going after Jeff." She said she didn't know what happened—that we all used to be such good friends. I noted that the Quinns may have been good friends with her son and Monica, but certainly not me, and that our relationship was irrelevant to the story.

To print or not to print? I consulted with a few journalism gurus and spoke with Las Vegas attorney Dominic Gentile, who was contemplating action on behalf of Colton Guinn, who was also claiming financial wrongdoing by his father.

I decided to proceed. The story posted to my blog on October 13, 2016.

Police investigating child sex abuse allegations against Gov. Guinn's son, daughter-in-law

Metro Police confirm they are "actively investigating" allegations of

The Anointed Son

child sex abuse against Jeff and Monica Guinn, the son and daughter-in-law of former Nevada Governor Kenny Guinn. No charges have been filed.

The Guinn's son, Colton, now 24, alleges in police reports that he was the victim of sexual abuse at the hands of his parents from the age of four to 15 years and suffered physical abuse from the age of four to 22 years.

Colton Guinn told police he was sexually abused 30 to 40 times between 1996 and 2007, during the time Kenny Guinn was governor.

Former First Lady Dema Guinn, who has been interviewed by a Metro Sexual Assault detective, spoke with me by phone about her grandson, who she referred to as "our problem child."

"He just wants money," Mrs. Guinn said of her grandson. "He wants to live the lifestyle they used to have. He thinks Jeff and Monica owe him $3 million."

"Colton wasn't raised right," Mrs. Guinn said of her grandson's upbringing. "He was rewarded for bad behavior. It wasn't how Kenny and I wanted him raised."

In a series of police reports filed with Metro Police in April and May of 2016, Colton Guinn details the alleged abuse and says he is being harassed, followed and threatened by his parents because he reported the allegations.

"...they keep trying to get a hold of me and threatening myself and my girlfriend/family with the cops," he wrote in a police report.

Colton's father, Jeff Guinn, has a history of co-opting police to do his dirty work and having his foes followed. Colton Guinn says his father brags of having "cops on the payroll."

Jeff Guinn is currently standing trial in federal court in a civil *bankruptcy fraud case stemming from his failed hard money lending brokerage, Aspen Financial.*

(Note of disclosure: From July 2015 through March 2016 I did part time paid investigative work for the Plaintiff's attorney, Dennis Prince.)

Attorney Dominic Gentile confirms he's been hired by Colton Guinn but won't identify the issue, only that it's "personal business."

Gentile calls the matter "a very sensitive situation."

Gentile notes he has not filed a lawsuit on Colton Guinn's behalf and may not be forced to make a public filing.

"If it's a thing, and I'm not prepared to say that it's a thing at all, it's possible, given the very sensitive nature, that we could avoid filing a lawsuit. Do I believe him? Absolutely. But me believing him and proving it are two different things. I'm going to be awfully cautious," Gentile said.

Jeff Guinn screamed at me to get away from him when I approached him during a break in his trial to ask about his son's allegations. His wife, Monica, hung up on me and did not to respond to a text requesting a response to the allegations.

Metro police have not responded to my recent requests for an update. No charges have ever been filed against Jeff or Monica Guinn.

Colton Guinn says he was unable to pay the legal retainer necessary to proceed with legal action.

83: JUSTICE DELAYED?

"Your Honor, this case started out seven years ago. And in April of 2009 the Ruthes filed this action against Mr. Guinn and Aspen Financial Services, seeking to hold him accountable for all of the harm and the loss that he caused through what we now know is a complex scheme to defraud them and it's been a long seven years.

And in the summer of 2013, Aspen Financial Services filed for bankruptcy. It had no assets. Mr. Guinn filed for bankruptcy in October of 2013. And many people have asked over -- my clients, myself, why continue on, he's bankrupt. Because this is a story that needs to be told."

-Attorney Dennis Prince, Opening Statement, Ruthe v. Guinn, September 26, 2016

Seven years. That's how long Donna Ruthe waited for her day in court. In the interim, she lost her father, and not long after, her husband.

Before Parkinson's Disease robbed Chuck Ruthe of the ability to communicate, he secured one promise from his wife: that she'd see the suit against Guinn to the end.

The long-awaited day began with a pronouncement from the Honorable Gary Spraker, a visiting federal judge from Alaska, who reminded Ruthe's attorney he had two weeks to present his case. The defense would have another week.

Prince's opening statement alone took two hours, culminating in a demand for $6.9 million.

Jeff Guinn looked disheveled, watching as Prince's PowerPoint presentation played out on the monitor in front of him, telling a story of unchecked greed that could only be sated by loan upon loan, each earning Guinn's Aspen Financial a fortune in fees.

With payments rolled into the loan, Prince explained, interest checks arrived in the mail like clockwork.

But good economic times gave way to bad, revealing a disastrous business model, which relied on ever-increasing appraisals, serial refinancing, and, inevitably, equity erosion.

What must Jeff be feeling? I wondered silently whether I could persevere under the weight of such stress.

A few dozen people filled the rows—far more than usual in bankruptcy court.

The Quinns were there to lend moral support to Ruthe, as were at least a dozen other friends and neighbors.

In summary, Guinn's defense consisted of the following:

- Aspen Financial was a lender of last resort.
- Lenders decided to invest in risky, highly speculative loans.
- No one could have predicted the economic recession.
- Ruthe made money. She has no losses.
- The Guinn family lost money.

Guinn's testimony was fraught with contradictions; among them, his denial under oath of his role as the primary underwriter of Aspen loans.

Dennis Prince: You were the lead underwriter?
Jeff Guinn: Oh, I don't know about that. That's your words. So --
Q: Do you agree that you were the lead underwriter?
A: No.
Q: Do you recall telling me you were the lead underwriter?
A: I don't recall. If I did, it probably wasn't correct.

The post-trial brief filed by Guinn details each loan transaction, noting the plaintiffs signed subordination agreements allowing Aspen Financial to act on their behalf. The lengthy brief fails to mention that in all but a handful of the loans at issue in the lawsuit, those critical documents, along with state-required disclosure forms, were signed after the close of escrow, and after the subordination had occurred, often in violation of the law.

The Anointed Son

This is from the post-trial brief filed by Aspen:

> ...neither Aspen nor Mr. Guinn can be accused of fraud or willful and malicious conduct simply because certain investors (i.e., the Plaintiffs) decided not to read and understand the Loan Officer Analysis, the Loan Summary and Investors Authorization, or the appraisal—documents that Aspen undisputedly provided to all investors, including the Plaintiffs, for each and every loan they ever funded at Aspen.

The brief ignored the salient fact that the disclosure information, with few exceptions, was delivered after the close of escrow and in violation of state law.

As far as I could tell, except for his attorneys, no one appeared in court to support Jeff Guinn during the three-week long trial—not his wife, Monica, nor his three sons, nor his mother, former First Lady Dema Guinn.

Closing arguments were held in December 2016 to accommodate the visiting federal judge from Alaska.

Attorney Dennis Prince argued Guinn's actions satisfied the requirements for a Ponzi Scheme.[125]

Jeff Guinn's attorney argued that among Aspen's thousands of investors, the Ruthes were lone wolves who erroneously blamed Jeff

---

[125] U.S. Code 523(a)(6) "A Ponzi scheme is an arrangement whereby an enterprise makes payments to investors from the proceeds of a later investment rather than from profits of the underlying business venture, as the investors expected."

In re Agric. Research & Tech. Grp., Inc., 916 F.2d 528, 531 (9th Cir. 1990).

§ 523(a)(6) requires: (1) subjective intent to injure, or subjective belief that harm is substantially certain to occur; (2) a wrongful act, done intentionally, which necessarily causes injury, without just cause or excuse; and (3) injury.

Guinn, rather than the Great Recession, for their losses.

As of this writing, two years since the trial began, the judge who rushed the attorneys to argue their cases has issued no ruling.

Is it odd for a federal judge to take so long to rule? Odd, yes. But not unheard of, as federal judges are under no time limit.

The verdict in the trial was to be the final chapter. Instead, the question of accountability has yet to be resolved, and this story has no ending.

Will Jeff Guinn, who overcame incredible odds to beat a federal grand jury investigation, be absolved of allegations of fraud?

Or will a federal judge from Alaska take action where Nevada regulators and federal prosecutors feared to tread?

Stay tuned.

###

Post-script:

In February 2018, Jeff Guinn re-entered the hard money lending industry as CEO of Battle Born Capital. The company's website boasts:

Jeff Guinn is a long-time Nevadan with deep family and business roots in the state he proudly calls home. Guinn is one of the true innovators and entrepreneurs of the hard money lending industry in Nevada, having grown his previous firm, Aspen Financial, to one of the largest hard money lending companies in the state. However size is nothing without quality: Aspen also received the highest marks awarded by the Nevada Mortgage Lending Division for the fourteen years of its operation. From that legacy and with the important lessons of the Great Recession, Jeff has sought to build Battle Born Capital into the highest quality and most trustworthy hard money lender in Nevada.

Guinn's partner is Amanda Stevens, an attorney who once worked for Guinn's attorneys, Bailey and Kennedy, and for another failed hard money lender, USA Capital.

The Anointed Son

The Nevada Mortgage Lending Division points out that although Jeff Guinn's corporate alter ego, Aspen Financial, had its license revoked, Guinn, the person responsible for Aspen's insolvency, has never been disciplined and has a valid and active license as a mortgage agent.

Makes sense to me.

Federal court records reveal Sean Corrigan entered into a negotiated agreement in 2018 with the FDIC to satisfy his $22.5 million judgment.

ABOUT THE AUTHOR

Dana Resnick Gentry is a native Las Vegan, mother of four, and award-winning investigative TV reporter. She is the Senior Reporter for the Nevada Current, an online news site. Dana lives in Henderson, a suburb of Las Vegas, with her husband, Larry, three dogs, three cats, and a noisy cockatoo. Some of Dana's work can also be found at danagentrylv.com

Made in the USA
Middletown, DE
03 December 2018